W9-BGA-328

RED FLAGS
for Primary Teachers

Previously Published Works by
Katie Johnson

Doing Words

More Than Words

Reading Into Writing

RED FLAGS for Primary Teachers

27 Neurodevelopmental and Vision Issues that Affect Learning with Activities to Help

Katie Johnson

Foreword by
Dr. Len Press, D.O., FCOVD

Tendril Press™
DENVER, COLORADO

Red Flags for Primary Teachers
www.KatieJohnsonAuthor.com

Published by Tendril Press™ Denver, CO

www.TendrilPress.com 303.696.9227

Printed in the USA

ISBN: 978-0-9831587-8-3
10 9 8 7 6 5 4 3 2 First Publishing: 2013

Library of Congress Control Number: 2012941870

Cover & Author Photos:
Bronwen Houck,
BronwenHouckPhotography.com
info@bronwenhouckphoto.com
206.940.8662

Art Direction, Book Design and Cover Design

www.ajimagesinc.com — 303•696•9227
info@AJImagesInc.com

to

Carita

whose idea it was

Childhood is a journey, not a race.

—unknown

Contents

Section Two – *What I Do*

The amount of information given to teachers about

Photographs

Foreword

by Leonard J. Press, O.D., FCOVD, FAAO

The amount of information given to teachers about neurodevelopment or visual function in their preparatory coursework is close to nil. At first blush you might feel that is just as well, because teachers need to focus on theories of learning and matters of pedagogy. Downplaying the role of movement and vision in the educational environment, however, does children a serious disservice, and this marvelous handbook by Katie Johnson tells you why.

A Call For Action–

Coming from a clinical framework of developmental vision, I found myself questioning Katie's choice of the term "red flags" for signs and symptoms children were exhibiting that should signal concern. Clinicians are used to thinking in terms of risk factors, and these risks might then result in performance that is sub-optimal for a child's potential. The more I read, the more I realized that Katie's use of the term "red flags" was appropriate for what she was observing in the classroom. In fact, it was far better than to consider these behaviors as risk factors because Katie's message is a call for action.

How did we arrive at our current state of affairs in education? There are many teachers who are astute observers of individual learners, but who are consumed with satisfying metrics on which their own performance will be judged. The tendency therefore is to focus on lesson plans and mandated testing. A child who struggles to learn can easily fall through the cracks, particularly if he is not a behavior problem. It is not uncommon for parents to relate that they know their child isn't keeping pace with his peers, but that he does not qualify for support services because he isn't "bad enough". To wait until a child fails before intervening is unconscionable, but there is tension in balancing an increasingly tighter budget for available services.

Informed Observation–

Reading the handbook Katie Johnson has put together should inspire you to broaden your insight through informed observation. You will find numerous case examples of children who are going about their day-to-day learning in the classroom in a very inefficient manner. Katie is able to share her observations based on her explorations into BrainDance, Brain Gym®, and

Optometric Vision Therapy. The crunch on a teacher's time makes it seem a luxury to incorporate movement activities in to the classroom. The message here is that appropriate stimulation of the vestibular system during the school day, particularly during the formative early elementary years, is crucial in priming the child for learning during the school day.

Specific Guidelines and Activities–

Some of the children under your care will experience personal issues that will ultimately require referral to a professional. Raising concerns about a child can be a sensitive issue, but Katie lays out a template for when certain observations should be addressed through specific guidelines and activities she provides, and when professional intervention is required. A very important point is that there will be a number of times when you can begin to provide a child specific support through some very basic activities while at the same time educating the child's parents about the need to seek professional assessment and guidance.

Be an Advocate for Children's Visual Neurodevelopment–

For the past few years, I have been giving seminars to educators, occupational therapists, physical therapists, and speech-language pathologists on the role of vision in learning. At times participants will approach me during a break to advise me that they'd like to do more for children in this area, but that they're discouraged from doing so by their supervisors in the school setting. Now, to each of these individuals, I will be able to say: Read Katie Johnson's *Red Flags,* and you'll be inspired to be an advocate for children's visual neurodevelopment and all that it can do to level the playing field.

Leonard J. Press, O.D., FCOVD, FAAO
The Vision and Learning Center
Fair Lawn, New Jersey

Acknowledgements

Had I never moved to Seattle, had I never met Anne Green Gilbert, this book would never have been written or even imagined. As a dance educator, Anne is the most influential voice about the development patterns of children; she combines her understandings with working with children every day.

Had I never met Anne Green Gilbert, I would never have met Bette Lamont or anyone else who does neurodevelopmental therapy, and would never have seen and understood the reasons for the problems my students were having.

Had I never heard the words "vision therapy" from Anne and Bette, I would never have met Nancy Torgerson, whose work as a developmental optometrist makes me want to be one when I grow up…or in my next life.

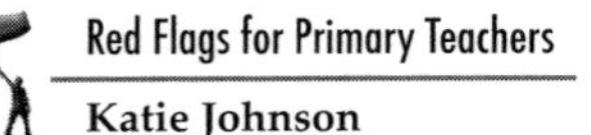

Had I not been dancing all these years, I would not have known Bronwen Houck, of Bronwen Houck Photography, whose photographs illuminate these pages.

Many thanks to all these strong and sensible women. The children I teach, the parents of those children, and teachers everywhere benefit from their work. I am grateful for their teachings and support.

Introduction

Have you ever had a child in your primary classroom who had no history or suspicion of any problems, and yet that child couldn't learn to read and write? He or she is the child from an ordinary family, with a middle-of-the-year birthday, who eats breakfast at home, who is the pediatrician's dream, who is well-behaved and trying to do his or her best in your classroom, and yet that child CAN'T?

All of my teaching life, I've had such children in first, second, and third grade. They've been fascinating and baffling. Over the years, I've made such statements as:

> "I can't put my finger on it, but something's not quite right with Derek."
>
> "Tiffani isn't working to her potential."
>
> "It takes Amina forever to finish her work."

"It shouldn't be this hard for Diego."

All puzzles. Why can't Derek, Tiffani, Amina, and Diego, perfectly smart children in first grades all over the country, learn to read?

It's not because they are from a non-English speaking household, although that does make reading and writing English more challenging than for a child who has parents speaking English. It's not because they are in a classroom of twenty-eight or more children, although that does make learning anything more difficult. And it's not because they're living in a residue of a messy divorce or the class is full of unruly children.

They have trouble with reading because they've unfinished vision or developmental patterning. Their eyes do not properly track across and/or down a page of print. They can't connect the shapes of letters with the sounds of letters. Sometimes they don't know there are two sides, left and right, as well as front and back of their bodies, and also there are two sides, left and right, of a piece of paper or a page in a book.

They may not be able to "cross the midline," that is, automatically move their eyes across the page or move their pencil-wielding hands across the page as they write. And there are times when they do not even know where their bodies are. As a result, they bump into people, misjudge distances, miss the chair they intend to sit on, or they have to touch the wall as they walk down the hall.

And it is not getting any easier for them.

The first twenty years I taught elementary school, I managed classrooms and instilled respectful behavior in children. I understood how to get children excited about reading, writing, and become competent in math, science, and art.

Children then…

My job centered on those subjects and the thousand other things six-and seven-year-olds need to know. I didn't know about unfinished developmental patterns or about how the eyes need to work in order to make sense of print. I didn't worry about too much time spent playing video games because most of my students didn't own them. My students hadn't spent a lot of time buckled into a car seat because most of my students' parents did what their parents had done: put the kids in the back of the pickup or the car.

I knew some children were slower, some students were very capable, and some students were just plain odd. I suspected some students might not have supportive home lives, adequate minds, well-balanced personalities, human kindness, or enough or too much intellectual challenge.

Part of my repertoire was using movement in the classroom because I believed that six-year-olds needed to move! I did sign language (ASL) with kids as an additional modality to explore while they were acquiring literacy. I loved to do exercises such as, "Head and Shoulders, Knees, and Toes," and dancing when each child held a letter card and made words with other children. When it was too cold outside to have recess, the kids would play *Simon Says.* I wore out several sets of records and tapes for movement and song by Hap Palmer, Raffi, and other musicians. I believed these exercises and activities were helpful, I knew they were fun, and I thought the children were usefully engaged by these activities. My problem—I didn't know why.

One way or the other, I taught them all.

And children now…

Today, we see in our children the fruits of more than twenty years of changes in parenting, how we see children, and the omnipresence of electronic media.

American children live restricted lives, constantly bound into car seats where they have to sit in one position for sometimes hours at a time. Most children don't go out and play without adult supervision, even in their own yards, because of parents' fear of sexual predators and kidnapping. From an early age, more children are spending their days in daycare centers where they are less likely to be held and encouraged to move about the floor and the room. Since 1994, fear of Sudden Infant Death Syndrome (SIDS) has created a panic about allowing a child to investigate the world on his/her tummy. The Back-to-Sleep movement has motivated this fear. Even with the prevalence of this movement, SIDS has not disappeared.

Images representing both fake and often frightening reality flash on large, small, and in-between screens, and they are accompanied by constant, and often startling, sounds. It's unusual if a household doesn't have, at least, one computer, iPod, television, video game, or something with a screen and noise. Many children have their OWN television, their OWN computer, and even their OWN iPod. In nearly every inch of stores and eating-places, even in the supermarket, screens flash advertising messages. Music pervades or invades many environments.

Computers are a feature of an infant's life, either deliberately in the form of programs purporting to teach or by default as a baby-sitter (even in licensed day care situations). How much damage can be done to the development of infants' and preschoolers' eye tracking and depth perception is a matter of debate. Many studies suggest there is a significant impact, which shows up later, as the child is involved with the schoolwork of reading and writing.

Technology is also growing in primary classrooms. School administrators expect teachers to give the children regular computer time, and they expect assessment of the children's learning, particularly in math, to be done on the computer. Some of these tests are timed, and they have no bearing or resemblance to the generally practiced math instruction in the classroom.

The bottom line—children are not the same as when I began teaching.

The organization of the body in order to read begins, believe it or not, at birth, and indeed, even before birth. An infant moves her head before she moves her eyes, watching her milk-deliver's approach. As she learns to focus on that person, she begins to make neutral paths called tracking. Tracking is essential to being able to correctly read and write across the page.

First, the infant learns to track horizontally when learning to move about and crawl on her tummy in her horizontal world. Then, she begins to creep on all fours while she raises her head, looking up and down, and learning to now track vertically. This activity integrates the vertical tracking and pulls the eyes into alignment. Later she'll look to her sides and in front of herself, lifting her head and moving her eyes as needed to see where she is going. She is beginning to track both ways. By the time she is five or six years old, her brain has made these vision abilities automatic. She will use them when she attacks print.

If crawling and creeping have not been part of a child's infancy, the child may well have academic trouble in school.

Wouldn't it be lovely if we could ask, "Did this child crawl around on his tummy as an infant? Did he creep on his hands and knees before he walked?"

Could we assume that a negative answer to those questions would tell us all we need to know? No. It's not that simple. A lack of a crawling and creeping experience won't explain a child's problems. In order to learn to cross the midlines of their bodies, to engage both the right and left hemispheres of their brains, and to allow their sidedness to emerge and consolidate itself, children must run, swing, and climb. They must be allowed to move.

For example, when they're seated in their car seats with their heads held in a static, forward facing position, eye tracking is discouraged. Moreover, other kinesthetic and tactile interactions with the world may be impossible or delayed.

When the sequence in how humans develop is incomplete, it will make learning in academic, social-emotional, and personal areas difficult.

After my second twenty years of teaching, I've begun to understand the source of the behaviors and learning failures that I observe in my puzzling and frustrating children. Each year, fewer of the children I teach have finished their developmental patterning and more and more of them have some vision problems.

Today, when I see red flags in children's behavior and performance, I know they're likely to be related to how they move or don't move, and how they see or can't see. I've collected and developed enough activities and strategies to try to help them as they struggle with print. Many times I can make a difference, helping them to move their bodies and their eyes to best advantage. Sometimes they need professional intervention. Routinely, I assume after years of observation, there is something slightly unfinished about nearly all children. They need some help, so they can do the work of school and life.

How to use this Book

- *Red Flags* is set up in a *Find Your Own Answer* format.
- Section One, *What I See,* presents the children with a description or story about the odd things reflecting unfinished development/ patterning and/or eye issues.
- Section Two presents the *Try This* strategies to improve or change the behavior.
- Section Three presents a distillation of what I've learned *so far*. There will always be more to learn and to understand about the brain and the body.

Section One
What I See

In this section I present the children's puzzling problems I encounter. They are presented alphabetically by problem. At the end of each problem description are suggestions for what to do next, offering activities and games that might help. Directions for the activities and games are found in Section Two. In addition to individual exercises, the entire class does BrainDance every day (see Appendix A).

Blurring and Doubling

To determine if a child's vision is blurred ask the question, "What do the words *do* when you're reading?" If you've guessed wrong, and the words are not blurring or doubling, the child will answer, "Huh?" If your educated guess is correct, the child will probably say, "Some letters are black and some are gray."

David Cook's book, *Why Your Child Struggles,* has solid examples demonstrating various ways a child might have blurred or double vision, but it doesn't display pictures that you might show to a child you suspect doesn't have clear vision. Nor does it do any good to ask the child, "Do you have blurred vision?"

Amina's Story—

In the spring of first grade, I asked Amina my question, "What do the words *do* when you're reading?"

She grinned, demonstrating with her hand, and said, "The words go up in a slant." Using her finger, she drew the slant line in the air. "They come back down, and some words are darker than others like when you use a fat marker instead of skinny one. They get fuzzy when the dark letters are on top of lighter ones."

Amina's description fascinated me. It indicated that she had a strong language ability to describe in such vivid detail what she was seeing when she tried to read. It was no wonder to me that she didn't want to read. Sorting through those blurred and fuzzy letters was exhausting to her.

What Do I Do Next?

If you have a child exhibiting similar challenges as Amina, go immediately to Professional Intervention.

Body—Side Pattern Too Long

In September, when we begin BrainDance work (see Appendix A), there are usually two to five children that only can only do knee-smacks on the same side. For example, the right hand smacks the right knee and the left hand smacks the left knee in front of their bodies. The children are able to perform cross-lateral knee-smacks in the front of their bodies by Halloween. Almost all the children.

Ira's Story—

In first grade, Ira was diagnosed on the autism spectrum, and to me that might be both the chicken and the egg. One of the hallmarks of autism is difficulty in connecting with others. He had difficulty making eye contact, whether with a child or adult. He was nervous and giggly with his partner when working in pairs. He avoided reading with anyone but me.

Since cross-lateral patterns strengthen social connections, I hoped this would improve both his neurological development and social abilities. Being with Ira felt circular.

Ira showed improvement, as the year progressed, which I attributed to his growing accustomed to our routines. After some months, he could do one movement cross-laterally—he could cross his midline with his hands to his shoulders or if I did it with him, he could reach down to touch his opposite toe. Right up to the last day of school, Ira never succeeded in cross-lateral smacks either in the front or the back of his body.

Every little bit helps, and by the middle of second grade, Ira displayed more confidence.

What Do I Do Next?

Try Back to the Wall, Scarecrow, and Spiderman while you hope for Professional Intervention.

Covering One Eye

When I read with children individually, I'm able to see how each child is interacting with the printed page. I almost always sit across the table from the reader with a book between us. This technique has three advantages:

1. I can see the rest of the classroom and what the other children are doing;
2. I can track the words from above with a finger or a marker, so the text the child is going to be reading is not obscured;
3. I have a clear view of what the child is doing with his eyes. I can see immediately when a child is not using both eyes.

Darnell's Story–

Every day, I make time to sit across the table from Darnell with a book between us.

"I can ride," he slowly reads, with a second or more between each word. Before reading the word, ride, he looks at the picture of the child riding the bicycle with her dad holding on the back of its seat. As he begins the next line of print, his left hand rises to his face. The fingers stroke his left eyelid once, then remain poised on his eyebrow, covering the eye. His left elbow sits on the table supporting the hand.

"I can ride with my dad," he reads aloud, and the hand remains on over the eye.

My finger is tracking above the words he's reading, and his right hand is holding the book. He goes on with the page or two I intended for him to read that day. When he is finished, I congratulate him on doing well.

"Does your eye hurt?" I ask.

His eyes widen, and he is startled. "No," Darnell says.

"Does it help you to read when you cover your eye?"

He nods in agreement.

"What does it do?" I ask.

He shrugs. "I don't know," he says. I'm confident that he just doesn't know.

Shala's Story—

Shala comes to the task of reading, sitting straight, having the book flat, knowing what page she is on, and knowing where to start. After a few words, though, she begins to lean forward toward the table, and her right hand rises to her face, covering her right eye. As she continues, word by halting word, she is only using her left eye for the task.

During the first few months of first grade, it isn't easy for me to tell whether Shala is getting used to the idea of reading and experimenting with how to access the page. Or there is a string of other possibilities: she is starting a bad habit of leaning on her hand; or the whole event and process of reading is too exhausting; or she is only using one eye to read or see in general.

What Do I Do Next?

Covering the eye when he or she reads is one of the biggest red flags for me as a teacher.

As far as I know, the *why* has two possibilities.

The first possibility might be a tracking issue, which must be addressed to avoid long-term academic struggles. Not knowing where you are on a page of print will inhibit your reading speed, known as fluency, as well as processing speed in general.

The second possibility might be a teaming issue: one eye is being suppressed and/or seeing double. (It can also be true of adults who have no idea they are only using one eye.) This is the least desirable explanation.

If the result is that the child does learn to read and to do schoolwork without suppressing or not using one of his/her eyes—great.

Try Eyeball, Finger, Tracking, and Professional Intervention.

Crawling

When I first began working on movement issues with kids, I was only working with the kids needing reading help in K-4. At that time, I hadn't heard of vision issues, and I couldn't spell proprioception, let alone define it. Yet, the first few Kindergarten kids I worked with it certainly had vision issues and astonishing movement patterns.

Nicky, Ben, and Jason (all boys, I noted), couldn't cross anything (Ben couldn't even clap), didn't know they had a back to their bodies, had a great line in smiles and please-the-teacher behaviors, and no success in any part of reading.

I read *to* them, and I asked them to crawl. They smiled and stood there, so I got down on my tummy and crawled across the linoleum strip myself, while they watched, each one of them smiling at me. They tried crawling one at a time.

The Boys' Stories–

Ben was the most interesting to watch, as he'd lie on his side on the linoleum strip, scrabbling with his hands and feet. Surprisingly, he actually could move along the linoleum strip that way, although that posture is developmentally primitive. Nicky, a roundish child, balanced on his stomach with his feet straight out behind him, his arms straight out in front of him, and kind of inch-wormed his stomach across the linoleum strip. Jason simply pulled hard with his hands, his arms flat and his legs still. It took him a long time to reach the end of the linoleum strip.

What Do I Do Next?

We started with Back to The Wall, Knee Smacks, and Crawling. Later, when they had gotten an inch or two closer to reading, the boys crawled across the linoleum to match pictures with letters.

Crossing The Midline

Because human beings are bicameral, that is, two-sided left and right, they can walk in a cross-patterned way: left foot and right arm are moving at the same time, then right foot and left arm are moving at the same time. This alternating pattern allows us to balance, and it allows us to read. In order to read, human eyes must cross the midline of their bodies, as they track from left to right and back again. The wiring in our brains crosses a neutral pathway between our hemispheres called the corpus callosum, allowing us to track information across from one side of the brain to the other side of the brain.

When children put letters onto a page on one side only (but only with one hand), and seem unable to continue across the middle of the page, they are not aware of the midline of their bodies nor are they clear of their sidedness. Also, it might mean they are only able to see out of one eye, and they are working with only half of their normal visual field.

I wish I had known more about eyes when I was working with Julia.

Julia's Story—

Julia was a first-grader. She was the first child I saw not crossing her midline. When Julia wrote—strings of random letters—she used her left hand for her marks on the left side of the page, and her right hand for her marks on the right side of the page. Usually Julia made a few on one side, and then made a few on the other side. Then, beaming, she'd want to read the marks to me. She had no sound-symbol correspondence, even for the letter *J*. She wrote only her name in the right order of letters, on the right side of the paper, and with her right hand. This preference was my only and very weak evidence that she was right-handed.

What Do I Do Next?

You might try: Knee Smacks, Other Half, and Tracking. But surely Professional Intervention is needed for such a child, either in movement or vision. Julia might have been helped in a small way by Spiderman if I had been aware of the exercise at the time she was my student.

Elbow Crawling

I've discovered most five and six-year-olds that are academically the least able are often the least able to belly crawl. At the age of six, these same children can't skip. But, it still amazes me that Kristen was very academically and socially together but still couldn't do it. Some accomplish many academic and social activities with no problems, and yet, they can't do a cross-pattered belly crawl.

Kristen's Story–

Kristen had a November birthday. She was at the best age for first grade; she was a natural leader, whom her classmates looked up to and trusted, and she was doing good first-grade work. She was the kid who could have taken over if no substitute had appeared. She confidently performed BrainDance every day, but when I got out the linoleum strip once a week for the entire group, she was a surprise.

At first, Kristen did what I call Army Arms. In other words, Kristen would reach out with her elbows to propel her upper body along the linoleum strip. Usually, Army Arms are accompanied by one-legged propulsion with the other foot dragging behind. This is a common though incorrect crawling pattern for six-year-olds. Amazingly, Kristen's feet were neatly poised up in the air above her bent knees.

Watching her, it was obvious to me that she was a beautiful Lego® building with missing Lego® pieces in its foundation.

What Do I Do Next?

With Kristen's class, I knew enough to go back a pattern if the child seemed unfinished. I also added in KNEE SMACKS and other cross-lateral patterns.

Kristen did a lot of body-side, such as THE SCARECROW and SWINGS AND BEARS. Now when I have kid like Kristen, I will also have him/her do SPIDERMAN.

Eyes Really Close

A child's body may be well coordinated, he may remember all the routines and schedules of the day, and he will typically remind you of unusual events for the day. The child may be on Attention Deficit Hyperactivity Disorder (ADHD) medication, which in the case of Lewis kept him quite charming.

Lewis' Story—

Lewis couldn't learn to read. He could keep the whole schedule in his head, but he couldn't decode words, he couldn't tell the letters apart, and he couldn't remember the common high-frequency words. He lowered his head close to the paper or the page, he tracked each letter and each word with his right index finger, and he miscalled nearly all of them.

It didn't seem to matter how easy the text was, nor whether he was trying to read his own writing. He was a great role model and a neat kid, but reading did not happen for Lewis.

As the year went on, Lewis became more anxious. His parents had him fitted for glasses for seeing at a distance, which naturally didn't do anything to help his ability to read. We did a lot of work with phonics and phonemic awareness, which, slightly more surprisingly, didn't help his ability to read.

Lewis operated on memory, context, and excellent guessing.

What Do I Do Next?

Try to persuade the parents to get Professional Intervention. While you're waiting for the intervention, try Scarecrow and Eyeball.

Falling Out of the Chair

It is always unexpected when a child falls out of his chair onto the floor. It doesn't happen too often, maybe one child every five years or so, but it is very disconcerting. A child in your classroom might fall off his or her chair several times during the course of the day. A teacher's first reaction is that the child is being goofy. But such children don't fall off a chair to elicit giggles from classmates or to annoy the teacher. They simply can't help it.

Harry's Story—

Harry was a slightly built, sweet, pleasant, friendly, kind, gentle blond boy in kindergarten. Sometimes, he ambled into the classroom with his backpack falling off his shoulder or his jacket hanging from his hand. Usually his mother walked behind him and carried all his stuff, putting it away while Harry greeted friends and looked for his chair. His chair was located at the end of the table, near an empty space in the room. It was important for Harry to have space around his spot in the room because during the course of a school day, he often fell off his chair and onto the floor. The other children often giggled, which only made things worse.

Harry, Areielle, Matthew, Ben H, and Monique fell off chairs because they only had an indistinct idea of where they were in space, and their vestibular systems were fairly primitive. Their reflexes still prompted them to wriggle and continually readjust to contact with their chairs.

After falling off his chair in kindergarten three to four times a day, Harry came to me in first grade. At the end of the previous year, he had been given a vest to wear in the classroom, with sand sewn into the pockets to help him stay in his place and to know where that place was in relation to his body. In first grade, Harry put it on the chair when we did BrainDance or other exercises. Gradually, his falling episodes lessened, and he fell off the chair only once a month or so.

What Do I Do Next?

Try BEARS, LOG ROLLING, and as much tactile stimulation as you can find. A child like Harry needs to work with a neurodevelopmental therapist. Harry would have done well sitting on a ball or swathed in a hanging LYCRA® hammock.

Head-Moving

Knowing what is on either side of you is essential when walking, running, driving, and performing other activities. It's helpful to turn your whole head to see things that are situated to the right and to the left of your body. When you're reading, however, turning your head is an unnecessarily large movement, which doesn't serve you in a positive way as a reader. One of the things a reader must do is to track words from left to right across a page, interpreting the black squiggles as letters which make sounds, and then make words in some indefinable way inside the brain. But the page isn't wide, and moving our heads as we read is, at the very least, inefficient.

Valerie's Story—

Valerie is a tall, self-contained, slightly shy child. It is only September, but I spot a red flag. Valerie is appropriately tentative, as she reads a simple repeated book. She is reading, as opposed to reciting a book she has previously learned. The red flag: she is moving her head from side to side using her whole head to track the words.

It's not a terrible thing to move your head if you're five or six years old, but it's a poor habit to develop. Every year, Valerie will be required to read more in school, and moving her head from side-to-side will make her tired, and soon, reading will not be fun. Also, she will not be fluent enough, as moving her head requires more time, and she must learn to read faster to keep pace with the material being taught to the class.

I want Valerie to concentrate on keeping her head still while she reads. She is to move only her eyes, as she reads across the page. Her eyes must learn to move independently from the movement of her head. I will routinely do exercises with her, as she reads with me, and I'll convince her to keep her head still and move only her eyes to track the print on the page.

What Do I Do Next?

Try EYEBALL, FINGER, BEANIE BABY®, and OTHER HALF.

No Back

More than half the children starting first grade can't do cross-lateral foot smacking behind themselves. Most of these children can't do tactile movements up the backs of their bodies. Cross-lateral connections in back of your body are harder because you can't see what you're doing behind yourself, and perhaps you do not even know you have a back.

Adrienne's Story–

Adrienne had a summer birthday. She was a dreamer, an artist, an eldest child in her family, and she was on a soccer team, often at the wrong end of the field. She preferred to focus her attention on lizards and possessed a good deal of information about them. She had friends, but I thought she was surprised when she actually talked, played, and worked with them.

She slowly and dreamily moved through the day not finishing assignments because she'd get sidetracked into and stuck in an illustration. As far as I could tell, her problems were not vision related; she just wasn't "there" some of the time.

As hard as it is to assess, I assumed Adrienne's tactile and vestibular systems weren't as complete as they needed to be. Having a summer birthday, perhaps she wasn't as mature as many of her classmates.

What Do I Do Next?

Try Tactile and Log Rolling, in addition to BrainDance. And waiting!

Reversals

Except for spelling, nothing worries parents more than reversals. I'm not concerned about reversals until a child becomes fluent in writing or math. After all, most children are still working on fine-motor skills, such as printing letters and drawing recognizable objects well into the first grade when they are six and seven years old.

More puzzling to parents than letter reversals are number reversals. Over the years, many parents have asked me, "Why is Gary or Susan still making the number five backward? There aren't very many numbers to learn!"

"True," I respond.

There are only eight numerals susceptible to reversing. It's hard to make one and zero backward. For this reason, my favorite number is eleven. "In the first grade," I tell parents, "kids have been messing around with letters since they were three, or sometimes two, trying to write their names. Numerals have not been interesting to them, and as a result, they don't pay attention to them until they're in kindergarten. They haven't practiced them as much as they've practiced their letters. Let's not get concerned until the child is in third grade, and there is still a problem with reversing."

Letters are more difficult, especially, the ones with similarities in their formation, such as: *a, b, p, d,* sometimes, *q,* and the *g* with the candy cane stem. There are 52 of these things because only *o* is hard to mess up, but there are two sizes of that one! Lower-case *q* is blessedly rare in kindergarten and first grade, so, we mostly have *a, b, c, d, p,* and *g* to fuss about. Not to mention *s*—let's not mention *s*.

Sophia's Story—

I expect reversals of some letters for the first half of the year. I expect reversals of the worst six letters until a child is writing more than one page of continuous text, which is usually 25 to 35 words, every day, in their writing time. (See *Doing Words,* Chapter 10—Orthography and Other Conventions). Then I expect none, and I accept none. Almost every day in the spring, I'd say, "Great story, Sophia." She was my most artistically and socially together student. I'd conclude by saying, "Please turn your *d* around."

"Where?" she'd ask. Then, she'd read the story aloud to me and find the *b* for *d,* or I'd read the sentence to her and she'd fix the reversed letter. By this time in the school year, Sophia and the other children understand capitals and periods, and they can readily read what they've written.

Sophia would always agree with me, and say, "Okay!" Oddly enough, Sophia never reversed the *p* in her name. Perhaps it's not odd, since she'd been writing her name for probably five years, as she was the youngest of five children, and many of her siblings played school with her.

It's very common for students to reverse their *b* and *d*, and there are mnemonics to help remedy the reversal of these two letters. Often, children are taught to think of "bed" and use the headboards and footboards as sticks of those two letters.

Except in her name, Sophia's big problem was with *b* and *p*, a much bigger red flag, because the lowercase letters, *b* and *p*, can be both horizontally vertically reversed. She not only mis-wrote *b* and *p*, she misread them. And because she couldn't see them, she couldn't read them.

What Do I Do Next?

Try Eyeball, both ways, Letter Practice, Other Half, and Scarecrow.

Skipping Words Horizontally

Horizontal tracking is a basic requirement for reading. (Also see TEARS WHEN TRACKING). If your eyes do not readily and steadily move across the lines of print, your brain can't make sense of them. Pay attention to kids skipping words, as they read across the line of print on a page.

Aric, Jack, and Amy's Stories—

Aric skipped words, as he read across a line of print and down a page. Routinely, he skipped one or two words on every line. Aric and others thought they were correctly reading, but they grew discouraged when corrected, and they no longer wanted to read. Sometimes, their eyes hurt so much, they'd cry.

When it was time to do silent reading, these children would avoid the exercise. Most of them would dutifully select books from the library, but they'd only look at the pictures. Jack and Amy were very good at looking at pictures, and they could perfectly retell the stories without reading the words.

They weren't tracking the words across the page, mostly because the muscles behind their eye-sockets were weak and not accustomed to working. They needed practice moving the eyeball from side-to-side in order to see the words.

What Do I Do Next?

If the inability to horizontally track comes from lack of practice reading (after all, they are beginning readers), tracking practice will help strengthen the muscles and make reading easier. If tracking practice for a month or two doesn't work, refer the child to a developmental optometrist.

Use Eyeball, Finger, Vertical Tracking and Professional Intervention.

Skipping Lines Vertically

Although tracking across the page is the first consideration of reading, tracking down the page is also essential. When a reader comes to the end of a line of print, where does she go? And if she can't go the next line, it'll make no sense.

Amelia's Story—

Amelia was in the second grade and this was her problem. She couldn't reliably read the stories that she needed to read. And, she was a classic case. Amelia had a good mind, great ideas, a nice personality and disposition, good family, caring parents, and older brother who didn't bully. What more could anyone ask?

Abruptly, Amelia stopped reading. Immediately, I realized that I hadn't been listening.

"That doesn't make sense at all," Amelia said. With indignation, she looked at me. Actually, she looked more puzzled than indignant. She had been reading P.D. Eastman's book, *Are You My Mother?*

"Read it again," I said.

"The baby bird looked up. He looked I did have a mother," she read. Again, she looked at me. "It doesn't make sense."

"I think you've skipped a line," I gently said. "Let's read it together." I put my finger above the words, and she read them, including the words in the line she had previously skipped.

"Now it makes sense," Amelia said.

Yes, I thought, *when you see the words, you can read them. But if you don't see them, you can't read them.*

For two years, her mom and I had worried this bone. Amelia had done the exercises I asked of her, and she could exquisitely crawl. I was at a loss as what to do next.

One day, her mom arrived to pick up Amelia, but she was still at afternoon recess. Mom looked tired and discouraged. I knew she had an odd ailment that required medical attention, but I had never asked about any particulars of this issue.

"How are you doing? You're looking tired.," I said.

She sighed. "'I've tried a lot of doctors to treat my headaches. Today, I had a session with my therapist, and she thinks I should be doing some vestibular exercise like you have Amelia doing." She grinned. "Maybe Amelia should see my vision therapist."

Bingo!

Mindy's Story–

Mindy was tiny, young for her grade, and very nervous. There wasn't much ADD diagnosis when she was in first grade or perhaps I would have started there. She couldn't sit still, and her eyes roamed all over the page. We made some progress with her ability to read by using a piece of card with a slit in it, just the size of a line of print, and she read only the words she could see in the slit. It was cumbersome, and it required an adult to move the card up and down the page. And, she was twitchy.

In third grade, it emerged that Mindy was being sexually abused, all the time, by an uncle. No wonder she didn't, couldn't, and wouldn't focus on reading. Maybe she didn't have any vision problems at all!

What Do I Do Next?

Start with VERTICAL TRACKING, OTHER HALF, TWIRL AND POINT, and PROFESSIONAL INTERVENTION.

Tears When Tracking

There are way too many screens in the lives of children now, more every day and even in cars! At the very least screens truncate the visual field; at worst, and most commonly, their width does not require the eyes to move much at all. As a result, muscles behind the eye sockets become weak.

Jack's Story—

Six-year-old Jack has barely begun to read. His mental imagery world is filled with Star Wars, Dinosaur Training, cartoons, or Wii® games. I'm sitting with Jack and realize he's not getting the idea. When he's watching screens, his eyes and his brain are receiving the images and ideas, and his sense of hearing is also engaged by music, noises, or by the figure's speech on the screen.

When he is watching the screens, his eyes do not have to shift very much to see what's happening, certainly not as much if he was walking in the woods, running in a field, or playing jump rope with a friend. When he's watching, there's no particular order he must use to make sense of what he's seeing.

In a printed book, although there may be pictures, they don't move so they may not be interesting to a child like Jack. And the print, which should not be moving, is full of letters—letters that Jack is unsure of. As he looks at the letters, he must identify them, connect them to their sounds in his mind to make words, recognize many of the smaller ones, and create meaning. There isn't any sound to help him.

When he's reading, his eyes have to move in a certain way to get the print into his brain, in order for it to be decoded and understood, move in specific sequence, left to right, from the top of the page to the bottom. He hasn't used the muscles that make these movements happen, and they hurt. Jack's eyes will tear up, just as his legs would ache if ran laps for the first time without stopping.

What Do I Do Next?

Try anything that will get Jack focusing and tracking. First try Beanie Baby®. Then try Twirl and Point and Paper Clip Pick Up, but also try other activities such as running on a line and that will help him to move his eyes in more directions than simply at a screen.

Toe Walking

I have seen a total of five toe-walkers in the primary grades. A toe-walker is unmistakable—the eponymous name says it all. Amongst mainstreamed children, this seems to be more of a problem in preschool and pre-kindergarten. According to Melvin Kaplan in his book, *Seeing with New Eyes: Changing the Lives of Children with Autism, Asperger Syndrome, and Other Developmental Disabilities Through Vision Therapy,* elementary school aged children who are on the autism spectrum are more likely to be toe-walkers.

Olivia's Story—

In 1975, I met a toe-walker named Olivia. This was long before I knew about developmental patterns.

At first glance, I thought Olivia was practicing ballet steps, and my first reaction was to tell her to stop. She could stop. She would walk on flatter feet, but she couldn't do so without giving it considerable thought. I moved from exasperation to acceptance, but I remained puzzled. At that time, I had no interventions to offer to help Olivia remedy this problem.

With all toe-walkers that I've known, it was never an affectation—they weren't trying to be a ballerina.

They didn't realize they were moving in an odd way. They didn't know they were not grounded and normally engaged by gravity.

What Do I Do Next?

I'd begin with BrainDance if I were to have another Olivia, and I'd also go to the SCARECROW, CRAWLING, and PROFESSIONAL INTERVENTION. It's possible that Olivia's vision development had been interrupted when she was very young in the precortical stage of development (See Section Three). Therefore, she was unsure where her body was in space (tactile and vestibular considerations). She also had not perfected her vertical tracking or, even earlier in her development, she had not perfected her depth perception in order to see the floor and determine where she was in relation to it. To this day, I often wonder what happened to Olivia.

Wall Hugging

In elementary school, there are a lot of lines. We line up and traipse down the hall to and from P.E., music lessons twice a week, and along the sidewalk outside the building to go to lunch each day. On Fridays, we move down and back one hallway to the library. Occasionally, we move down different halls to attend assemblies, other classrooms, and on different sidewalks for fire and earthquake drills.

It's an unusual group of first graders who maintain a straight line during any of these times. Frequently, the lines resemble moving worms or snakes in their tendency to curviness. The exceptions are earthquake and fire drills where the potential for panic keeps us in a straighter line. These are opportunities to observe the wall-hugging children. A wall-hugger *has* to touch the wall, as he or she moves down the hallway.

Helen's Story—

In all my years of teaching, I only had one wall-hugger—Helen. She needed to touch the wall, as she moved between different parts of the classroom. Helen always stayed close to the wall. Sometimes she trailed her hand along, as she walked to P.E. or recess with just her fingertips of her hand keeping in constant contact with the wall.

One day, I overheard Melissa talking with Helen.

"You're always touching the wall." Melissa bounced along beside Helen. "Let's go faster. We're going to be late!"

Helen moved to the middle of the hall, letting go of the wall but just for a second. I noticed her wobbling, then she swerved back to the wall. "You go! The wall makes me feel safe."

Marc's Story—

Many years later, I had Marc as a first-grade student. Marc was a loner, and as a result, he was never with anyone when he moved around the school. Often, by default, he was with me. He knew some of his letters, and he knew some of the sounds. He held his pencil in a slant in order not have to have too much pressure on the pencil. Letters slowly came onto the paper, and they looked weak and wobbly. He didn't care much about his work.

Marc could be sweet and charming to adults, but he was most often angry with other kids. He fell out of his chair once or twice a week, and he was often wan-

dering around when he should have been working or playing at something specific in a specific spot in the room. He displayed low muscle tone meaning that his muscles weren't operating effectively in relation to gravity, and/or that there was stress somewhere in his body, such as internal organs, muscles, and tendons. This would make it impossible for him to relax or "be" in his body.

Many of the papers he was supposed to have worked on were scrunched up inside the dark cave that was his desk. His pencils and crayons were strewn around inside and were impossible to find. Occasionally, he put his hands in the desk and stirred around. He couldn't find anything in it, nor could I.

Of all these issues with Marc, the one that shouted to me the loudest was that he was unclear where his body was in space. His "proprioception" was undeveloped. Often, he operated with his sense of touch—scrabbling in the desk, touching the wall—to connect himself to things. The other kids were either too close to him or he was too close to them. He didn't like either scenario and loudly voiced his objections. He needed as much help socially as he needed neurodevelopmental help. I didn't know which help was needed most. His parents didn't think Marc's problems were anything to fuss about.

What Do I Do Next?

For a child who has only a tentative idea of where he is in space, start with Back to the Wall, Scarecrow, and Crawling to connect his body to the floor; Log Rolling and Paper Clip Pickup might also help.

Wandering

Whenever you look over to check to see if he or she is working at an assigned activity either at a desk or in a group, the wanderer is somewhere else.

Your eyes circle the room, and you find the wanderer under your nose, or at the paper cutting table cutting something, or getting a drink, or with another group, or just rabbit hopping on the gray tiles at the back of the room. Occasionally, you can locate the wanderer by the grunting noises he or she is making when hopping.

Larry's Story–

Larry is an exceptionally consistent wanderer. He is almost never connecting with someone else, especially the other wanderers in the room. He is exclusively in his own head, and he is not above stepping on anyone who is in the way of his bounces, although he never does so on purpose.

When I go to him in mid-wander, and I instruct him to return to his seat, or to his work, even if his work is not at his seat, he's always agreeable and often surprised that he isn't in his place.

"Okay!" he'll say. Sometimes, he'll add, "Where am I?"

Where am I? is the real question. Where is he? Larry has no real idea where he is at any given moment. His proprioception is fuzzy. In a classroom filled with desks, children, activity, and expectations, Larry's inability to light or focus becomes very obvious. In a classroom of 25 children, there isn't much I can do except resist the temptation to talk to his parents about hyperactivity medication.

What Do I Do Next?

Start with TACTILE, LOG ROLLING, and SCARECROW. It might help to push his desk up against the wall to make his choices slightly more limited. He also will need some developmental movement therapy.

Wiggling and Twitching

When a child's neuropdevelopment is unfinished, it is hard for the child to stay still. If you don't know where you are in space (the definition of proprioception), you have to keep moving to check it out.

Sam's Story—

When I want to read to with Sam, he drags himself to the table. He starts by vertically holding the book with its lower edge on the table, puts it down flat, and backs up his chair. Then, he repeats the process. He looks at me, and I look at the book. He sighs, and I restrain myself from sighing too. He's a nice kid, but it probably seems to Sam that living on Mars would make more sense than trying to learn to read in my classroom.

The jury is out on Sam. It's possible that his body can't do two things at once, that is, sitting appropriately and holding up his head.

What Do I Do Next?

I will get him to move as much as I can, but it's best if PROFESSIONAL INTERVENTION with a neurodevelopmental therapist is in his future.

Words Falling into the Middle

The best way to know what is going on with a child's vision is to ask the child. Of course, the question may fall flat if you simply ask if his or her vision is blurred or the words jump around because the obvious answer is, "Yes. Doesn't everyone's?"

It's analogous to asking a color-blind person to find a particular color in the room—he or she doesn't see colors the way others do.

My best question is, "What are the words *doing* when you're reading? Do they move? How do they move?"

If your instinct is right, the child will say as Amina did (see Blurring and Doubling) when she said, "Some letters are black and some letters are gray." Or, "When I read, the letters move back and forth, and sometimes they slide into each other." These are the best answers because they tell you what the child is seeing.

Can you imagine how tiring and frustrating this is for the child?

Katharine's Story–

Katharine was a child who shouldn't have problems. Her brother, older by two years, was doing well in school, her parents were well-educated, her mom read to her, and she played all the games preschoolers play with colors, sounds, music, and movement. Katharine was smart and thoughtful, always contributing interesting and useful ideas to conversations and group work. Yet, she couldn't read and write. She grew increasingly discouraged.

We tried everything I knew how to do, and we were both frustrated. At the beginning of second grade, I told her mother that an outside-of-school eye exam would be a good idea. Her mother was non-committal. Then a death in the family occurred, and Katharine's problems were no longer central to the family's dynamic.

One day in the middle of second grade, we were reading the book, *Frog and Toad are Friends.* For no reason I asked out of frustration, "Katharine, what are the words *doing* when you're reading?"

Katharine's answer was immediate and clear. "The words are moving toward the middle of the book. They wiggle along ahead of me, and then they just fall into the place where the book is put together."

She pointed to the middle between the two pages. She looked at me with my mouth hanging open. "Don't they do that when you read?"

I contacted Katharine's mom, and she got her an appointment with a developmental optometrist's office. Within the month, Katharine began vision therapy. She felt much better about herself, and so did I.

How can you possibly know if a child has this problem if you don't ask?

What Do I Do Next?

For children like Katharine, PROFESSIONAL INTERVENTION is the best possible plan. Nothing I can do will hurt her; but nothing I can do is what she needs. Get the child to a developmental optometrist as quickly as you can before too much more valuable time passes.

Writing in a Triangle

The orderly placement of letters on the page is not a natural thing for fives and sixes. Most of them have to be convinced—gently—to put their letters and words in recognizable strings sitting on a line. Their writing paper comes with great variation in line width, but all teachers intend for children to print from left to right and top to bottom.

Marcie's Story—

Marcie is a terrific first-grader with elegant plots and sophisticated language. She is prolific, filling five or six sides of pages in her writing book every day.

In February, I noticed that her lines were creating a diagonally bisected page of printing every time, and I told her to return to the left side. She agreed, telling me that books do that, but then, she didn't. This triangle writing only appeared in her writing book, and not when she was writing about math or science or reading. I didn't worry, but still, it needed correction.

Jake's Story—

Jake's writing, while not prolific, went round-and-round the page, so that he was always writing right below an edge of the paper. Never mind that the lines he wrote on didn't do that. His letters were neat, in spite of the unusual use of space, but it was difficult for both of us to read. Yet, Jake didn't think this was odd.

The problem with the true triangle writer is that she or he may be suppressing the use of one eye (as possibly Shala was doing in the section, COVERING ONE EYE). After several days of worrying and marveling, I took the position that Jake was doing something else. He was doing something in a more experimental way.

What Do I Do Next?

The triangle-writer is fairly common, but I'd guess only about one in ten children is showing some signs of eye-suppression that will need intervention. Sometimes, as with Jake, waiting and watching may suffice.

First try SCARECROW and MARKER OUTLINE, and then try PROFESSIONAL INTERVENTION.

Yawning and Getting Very Tired

Nothing in the human body works without breath, and the brain needs more oxygen than any other part of the body (except the lungs). Some children just don't breathe well enough to send enough oxygen to their brains.

Parry's Story–

Parry was trying. His mother and brother, older by one year, were 100 percent behind him. They gave him all kinds of appropriate support (no more than one hour of video games support in today's world). Yet, Parry was still exhausted after about three minutes of reading with me. He would lower his head onto the table or place his hands on either side of his face, and drag his cheeks down with a huge sigh.

Christopher's Story–

Christopher wasn't trying too hard, as he had decided he wasn't good at this reading stuff. He was the youngest of five, and his mother was pretty tired of elementary school.

"He'll get there," she'd say, inserting cheerfulness into her voice. "His siblings are doing fine."

When Christopher read (or "read") with me, he'd yawn after about two sentences, and then he'd give me a pitiful look. "This is hard," he'd say, looking anywhere but at the page. It seemed to me that he might be better off reading while he was standing. Occasionally, we'd try reading while he stood, and he was a little more alert.

What Do I Do Next?

I suspect that these boys needed to do truly neurodevelopmental work and repatterning their systems before they could be finished.

Try TRACKING, EYEBALL, OTHER HALF and TACTILE, and suggest a developmental movement therapist to his parents for his treatment.

Section Two
What I Do

Introduction–

The activities outlined in this section are predicated on the idea that all the children are already doing the BrainDance (see Appendix A), and these specific interventions are in addition to that routine.

I've found it impossible to do all the suggestions every day, or even every week, with every child who needs the work. What I can do is often include small, two-minute, activities in the work of a reading or a math group. When I'm reading with an individual child, it is tempting to work a longer period of time. Large size classes have much to answer for. Often I had a portion of a paraprofessional or an aide's day when I first started using movement interventions. I would ask her to do the exercises, especially the ones that worked best in the hallway. In classrooms today, aides are few and far between.

I also use the help of parents. Parent volunteers can be trained to lead or monitor these exercises. It's not generally a good idea to have a parent monitor his/her own child, but there are exceptions. It's fun to see a parental ahaa when and if one occurs. This past year, Scotty's mother attended my class every Monday morning for an hour and a half, and she did eye-tracking exercise with seven children that had needs.

The exercises in this section are presented in alphabetical order, and they have all been referred to in Section One. I have no expectation that all the exercises will work, but none of them can hurt, they will be useful, and most of them are fun for the children. I suggest you keep track of what exercise you have tried with each child and record any success you can be proud of.

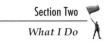

Back to the Wall

The first time I perform this exercise with a child, we sit with our backs against the wall. Together we raise our right hands and cross to touch our shoulders, elbows, cheeks, hips, knees, and toes, twice each time.

That's all there is to the Back to the Wall intervention. What's key to remember: repetition is important. After the first few days of working with the child, tell him he can do it himself, as it is much more positive for the child.

If the child gets pretty automatic as he sits with his back against the wall, ask him to stand with his back to the wall and do the same routine. After some weeks of standing and doing the exercise, he may be ready for skipping, which will move him away from the wall.

It's also helpful to do the Scarecrow at the same time.

BEANIE BABY®

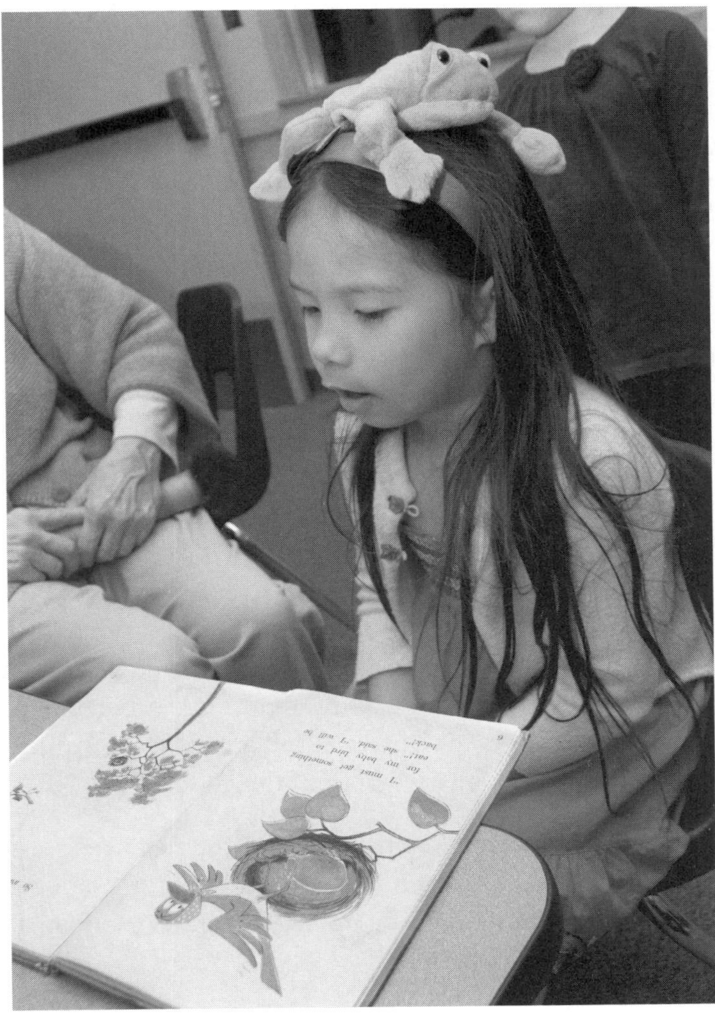
"I must get something
for my baby bird to
eat!" she said. "I will be
back!"
6

By age of six, a child should be able to track horizontally without moving the head. While you're moving a pencil back and forth across the child's visual field to check for tracking, or when he is reading, only his eyes should be moving.

If a child continues to move his head back and forth as he follows the pencil, first tell him he can't move his head. If he still moves his head, put a Beanie Baby® on his head to stabilize it. Sometimes (children older than seven years will get embarrassed), I'll use a beanbag instead. Any small, stuffed object will do, but my favorites are Beanie Babies® because they are the right size to balance on a primary head.

The first few times you ask a child to read with a Beanie Baby® on her head, she'll laugh and you'll know she's wondering if you're out of your mind. If she turns her head, though, the creature will fall off. Having the Beanie Baby® sitting on her head will build awareness of keeping her head still while reading. To become a competent reader, it's absolutely necessary to acquire this efficiency, the efficiency of not moving her head.

Sometimes a little pressure on top of the head helps—I'm unsure why. (If you have lice issues in your school, put the bean bag or the Beanie Baby® in a plastic bag overnight every night.)

Bears

Bears (and dinosaurs) most comfortably move in a body-side pattern, not cross-laterally as humans move, and of course both animals fascinate young children.

"Be a dinosaur" is a no-brainer successful request! Demonstrate by bending at the waist and walking across the available space (the hallway is a good place to practice this one) with the hand and foot of one side touching the floor at the same time, then the other side.

For variety, be a Papa Bear, or a Mama Bear, or a Baby Bear; or a Triceratops or Stegosaurus, or.... As the teacher, you make the decision whether or not these animals are threatening (loud) or sneaking up on something (silent).

Building a Match (Requires a partner)

Have two matching sets of six or so objects: red Unifix® cubes, blue rubber bands, big paper clips, small paper clips, hair clips, pennies, macaroni, etc. Keep each set in a separate Baggie®. Partners sit, facing each other at a table, each with a set. The first partner lays out a design with objects behind a moveable barrier (for example, a book standing between). Start with four of the things in the Baggie®.

Remove the barrier; instruct the partner to look at the grouping for some period of time (start with 20 seconds), then put the barrier back in place. The second player recreates the design of the first. Remove the barrier again, compare, and discuss. Emphasize the ways in which they are ALIKE! Switch roles. Each child should be the arranger of the objects four times.

Raise its difficulty by increasing the number of objects used; and then decrease the time allowed to look.

Bullseye (Requires a partner)

Straighten one section of a big paper clip.

Lay out six or eight different colors of Lifesavers® or Fruit Loops® in a line on a desk or a table, about one inch apart. The first partner calls out a color. The second partner holds the paper clip and tries to quickly plunge the straightened end into the hole of that color loop. Call all colors twice.

Change partners.

This exercise can get messy because the loops might fly around the desk if they're not hit in their holes. Increase the exercise's difficulty by calling out the colors faster.

Eyeball

Use any consistent item. I usually use one of the following: a pencil with a big eraser on the end or a two inch by eight inch strip of stiff paper with a picture of an eyeball pasted at the top of it.

Practice this exercise twice a day. Hold the item in front of the child's eyes about ten inches from his nose and slowly move it across his field of vision from right left and back again. Do this eight or ten times at each session. If the child can move the object back and forth, so much the better because it keeps his hands busy, and you can still see what his eyes are doing.

The child's eyes may tear up or sting; stop if they do, or if the child says they do, and repeat the next day. The problem is the muscles under the bones are weak, and they are not used to pulling the eyeball from side to side. Like all muscles, these will strengthen with use and the weepy eyes will diminish and disappear.

Watch to see if the eyes are in fact following the item. Repeat if not.

His head should not be moving. If it is, and "Keep your head still if you can," doesn't work, try the Beanie Baby® and the Finger.

If the eyes can't follow, or if they twitch back and forth, seek Professional Intervention.

FINGER (for Head Moving)

Sit across the table from a child who is reading to you and put your forefinger above the words she is reading. The distance the finger will move between the words is probably no more than half an inch, even with the fairly large print of first books. The tracking finger will focus her attention on the words, acting as a pointer, so she will read each word and her eyes will focus on the words below the finger, one at a time.

A finger is much smaller than the page is wide, and she will get used to moving her eyes across the small distance between the words, focusing on the words instead of the whole page. She will begin to move her eyes to see them. Occasionally say, "Keep your head still, please."

FINGER (for Covering One Eye)

During the day, watch a child to see if she turns her head to one side to look at other things, as well as the print. As she reads, ask her to track the words with the index finger of her right hand. In this way, she won't be able to use that hand to cover her eye. A red flag is evident if she continues to turn her head away from her reading, so that she is only using one eye. It will require vision therapy to correct.

Note on tracking: Beginning readers routinely use a finger or a marker to help them track words across a line of print; when they do this, readily without being reminded, and keep their heads still, rejoice! Every day, Amanda's reading is improving. She uses her finger to—her words—'keep her space'. Amanda is doing exactly what she needs to do. Soon she won't need to do this anymore because she is teaching her eyes to track the print all by themselves.

In the Hole (requires a partner)

Use an empty toilet-paper tube and a long straw or a blunt chopstick. One partner holds the tube while the other partner holds the stick. The tube-holder must be sure that the tube is positioned with its hole toward the other person, at chest level; the stick holder must keep firm hold of the stick.

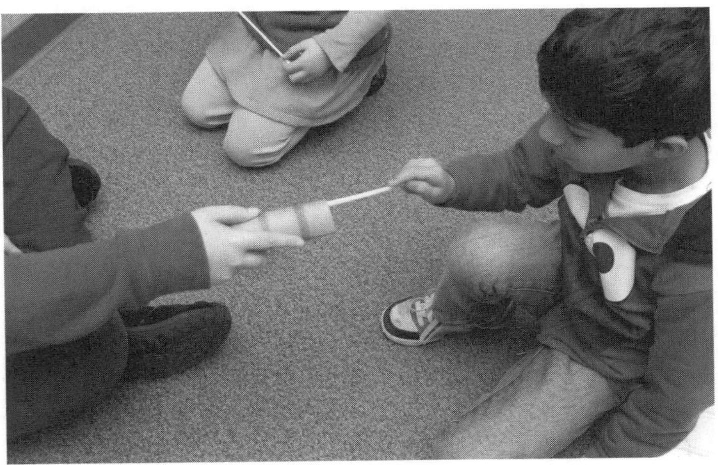

The tube-holder changes the horizontal position of the tube by a few inches so it's in a different spot, but it's still at chest level. At each new position, he holds it still so that the stick-holder can put the stick in the tube, and he can then quickly pull it out.

Putting the straw into the tube is a count of one. After completing nine times, they change roles.

You can increase its difficulty by making it faster, but be careful. Obviously this is an activity which aggressive children should not try or, if they do, they should be monitored.

Knee Smacks—(easiest)

To help the children balance and to eliminate the possibility of going backward, sit as many as four children, at a time, in the hall with their Backs to the Wall. The first few times sit with them. This exercise is like Back to the Wall. Next, everyone should raise their right arms and smack their left knees once. Finally, everyone should raise their left arms and smack their right knees once.

Repeat this exercise until they can't keep their focus on what they're doing. Sometimes, at the beginning, it's after only two smacks. Then do the same thing with opposite shoulders and then with opposite feet. At this time, leave them to do it by themselves.

If it seems easy, do the same thing with no teacher model; next, do it while standing. To make it more difficult, add forward motion. Demonstrate and then have the children move in a march with a right-hand-slap-left-knee and vice versa, around the room if the room is big enough, or up and down the hall if you can do that without disrupting anyone else.

(This is also helpful as a diagnostic activity to determine sidedness.)

Lazy Eights

Use a section of chalkboard at least four feet square and sidewalk chalk. Other chalk will work but the big kind is intrinsically more interesting. The child draws an "8" lying on its side (the infinity symbol), tracing and retracing it from the top right moving down and to the left. Trace over the same figure as many times as the child is old. The first day, use the dominant hand. The second day, use the non-dominant hand, and so on.

Clean the blackboard with a clean sponge so no traces remain. Keep the dark pink chalk out of the chalk container because that color leaves a permanent stain on a chalkboard.

Letter Practice

First try to ascertain if it is a fine-motor issue or a vision issue. (For a kid like Sophia, who had no fine-motor problems and sailed through CRAWLING and BrainDance, it was clearly a vision problem.) For a start, try any other medium to practice letter formation:

- sand on a cookie sheet with sides,
- shaving cream or whipped cream on a small board in a cookie sheet with sides, or
- simply water to wet the fingers and a small green-painted chalkboard (the least messy).

Have the child use the index and third finger together to make the letters, copying a card. (Those are the fingers that need to learn printing because they are the ones that hold the pencil. Add the thumb after a couple of weeks.)

Practice making and identifying letters with Play-Doh®, too. (It's great to have a small Baggie® of the stuff for each child.) Engaging a child's tactile connection to print with Play-Doh® can't hurt, so combining letter practice with phonics is a complete win-win, and fun besides. The child makes 3 short snakes about the thickness of a pencil and four inches long; ask her to make the word, say, "dog." (You make it too with your own Play-Doh®.) All with Play-Doh® put index and third fingers together below the *d* and slide them along below the word (sounding out if that's an issue too). Then say, "Change this word to 'dot,'" and continue. Change at least four times—cat, mat, mad, bad, for example. For every word, the child says the letters in the word, then sweeps his hand under the Play-Doh® letters from left to right, sounding it out, and then saying it again as he sweeps.

Log Rolling (Spinning)

A child can do this vestibular exercise by rolling as stiffly as he can across the floor. With his body straight, arms either down or up or both, he can roll his whole body the length of a ten-or twelve-foot linoleum strip about four feet wide, end to end every day, or as part of his vestibular pattern work in BrainDance.

This is a very tactile activity, and generally a pleasure for the spinner, but any spinning should be watched because it makes the spinner dizzy–a good thing for the brain, because it has to work to reorganize itself, but a bad thing if the spinner gets too dizzy and falls over.

Marker Outline

It's hard to be clear about what to do to help a child come back to the left side of the paper because there are many possible kinds of writing paper in the primary classrooms. You'll figure out what works best with your paper.

Use a dark erasable marker (like a Vis-à-vis®) to make a short, half-inch line at the beginning of every line the child should print on. Be sure he can see it, but use a different color if that seems called for. Tell him he has to begin putting the words of his story or other writing on the dark line. Ask him to touch that spot with his finger, followed by touching it with his pencil to show you he knows what to do.

Other Half

A picture showing half of something is printed on a quarter sheet of paper with room to finish drawing the other half. The child simply completes the picture. Amanda, of course, will want to color it too, which is fine.

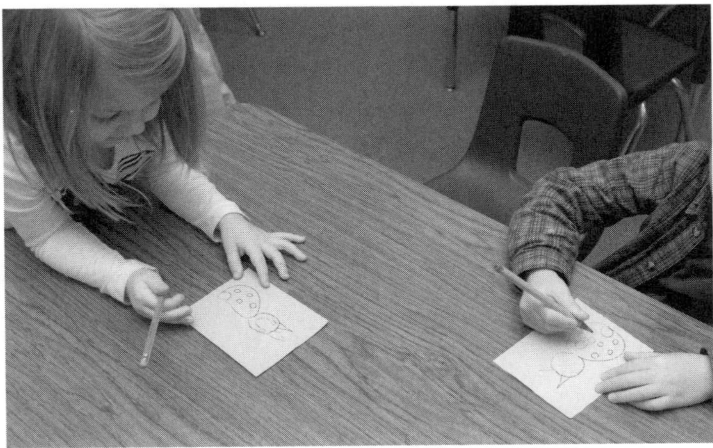

Paper Clip Pickup (Partner activity)

Straighten ten heavy paper clips. (Keep them in a small envelope—easier and safer than using rubber bands.) Vertically hold them in a bunch (one end of the bunch touching the playing surface) and drop them so they fall in a vaguely circular jumble, at least a foot across. The other person has to remove one without moving any others. If one paperclip moves, the player loses the turn.

It's a fun game for everyone, but it's most useful for those that need to focus and track or can't distinguish foreground and background (including finding important information in charts, etc., as well as seeing print against a background of pictures in early readers).

Professional Intervention

When you have identified a red flag requiring professional intervention, your usefulness to this child is over. The child needs the intervention of a developmental optometrist or of a developmental movement therapist, or both. (See Section Three)

Purple Balance

Use a paper-towel roll with a two-inch wide section removed, lengthwise, and the inside of the tube colored in three cross-wise sections, green, red, and purple with purple in the middle. The child holds the roll in her hand, open side up, trying to balance a Ping-Pong® ball in the purple section for a slow count of five.

Raise the difficulty by increasing the time to ten, or using the non-dominant hand, or balance the ball on one of the end colors.

This is primarily for focus, tracking, and a little bit for balance.

Rocking

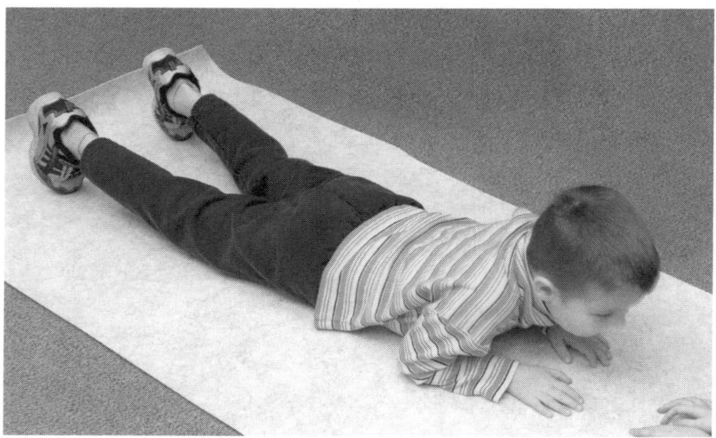

The child lies on the floor, on a smooth, wooden surface, or on linoleum, barefoot on her tummy. With forearms and the balls of her toes resting on the floor, she will push-and-relax with her toes beginning with one push/relax, per second, ten times; rest; ten times more. The goal is to work up to 40 rocks in one minute.

This exercise is designed to strengthen the feet and stretch the Achilles tendon. One cause of Toe-walking is there has not been enough belly crawling and the earlier stage of "rocking" has somehow been skipped.

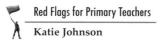

Another possible cause of Toe-walking is that the child had been trained to Toe-walk. Baby exercisers, such as

walkers and jumpers, may be examples of devices that unintentionally train toe walking. The 3 to 12 month old child sits, straddling a seat which hangs from a shelf around his waist. If the seat adjustment is too high the child pushes *with his toes* to move this contraption around the floor instead of the entire foot making contact with the floor. There is another jumper seat with a spring that hangs from a door frame in which the suspended child bounces against the floor with his toes. It has the slight advantage of being a vehicle for vestibular action, but the damage to the rest of the body vastly outweighs that advantage.

Same and Different

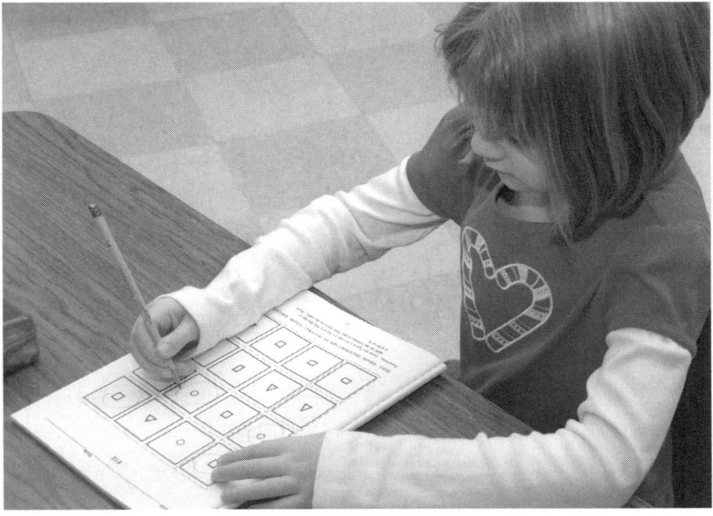

You may find any number of worksheets from a variety of reading, phonics, or penmanship programs, which requires a child to choose what words, letters, or pictures are the same or which require a child to identify what's different. These worksheets are best if they are set up in a right-to-left or up-and-down format.

The child should do one side (one worksheet) in each session. If you're able to time her, try to increase her working speed.

Scarecrow

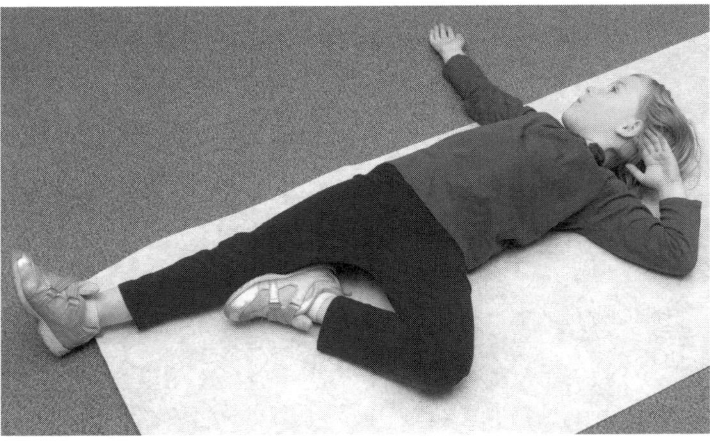

The official name of this exercise is: Tonic Neck Reflex Patterning. The first children who learned the exercise called it the Scarecrow. As you will see, the new name is quite descriptive!

The child lies on her back on the floor, with one arm stretched straight out to the side, and other arm bent so the fingertips touch the ear. The leg on the bent-arm side is also bent, toe-to-knee, making a triangle flat on the floor; the other leg is straight. The child's head is turned toward and looking at the fingers on the outstretched arm.

Have the child slowly move her head so she is looking the opposite way. As she does so, she straightens the bent leg and arm, and makes the other leg and arm into triangles. She is now in the mirror-image position of where she began.

It should take about two long seconds to switch. Have the child do the switch 12 or 16 times as one practice of this exercise. This solidifies the body-side pattern and begins to make a trail along the corpus callosum (See Section Three).

Spiderman

Some children get stuck in the Body-Side pattern, which should lead to the Cross-Lateral pattern. As Spiderman, the child can move laterally at first, then use arms and legs, alternating—right arm with left leg, left arm with right leg, in a truly Cross-Lateral movement. Some children will do this as a Body-Side activity for weeks or months and only come to Cross-Lateral

movement after they have had success for many days with the one-sided Spiderman.

The direction is simple and very engaging—who doesn't want to be Spiderman? I tell them, "Your job is to move like Spiderman does, going across the room as if you were going up a wall. Use your right hand and your left foot, then your left hand and your right foot. Go as far as you can in one direction, go back in the other direction. Do that twice the length of the linoleum."

There is a big Vestibular component to this exercise, because the head is almost upside-down as they move along the floor. If the space is big enough, the children could each have a section of wall and pretend to be Spiderman vertically. For most children this isn't as much

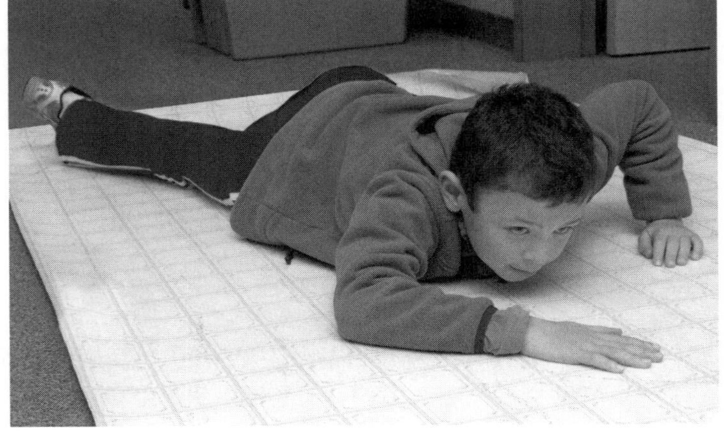

fun and, for me, it does not have the Vestibular component because the whole body is vertical.

Swings

Have the child stand next to the back of a chair with the seat turned away from the child. (You can also use a shelf or a doorknob provided it is at a height where the child can reach straight out to hold onto it.) Start with the child's left hand holding the chair back and the left leg standing in place. Have the child swing his right arm and right leg front and then back, front and then back, like a pendulum until he's done as many repetitions as he is old (if this is a second grader, that is probably eight). Switch sides and repeat with the left side swinging. Do the routine twice (for the second grader, twice is 32 swings).

To increase the difficulty, have the child do the swings slower or shakier or have him try swinging his arm to the front while the leg goes to the back.

After the child is good at this exercise, have him remove the stabilizing hand off the chair and try the exercise without holding onto the chair.

Tactile Work

When proprioception is unfinished, when a child is really not aware of where he is in space, nor even where his own body parts are, he needs more tactile work.

Begin with extra tactile pattern work in addition to daily BrainDance (see Appendix A). The child spends three minutes, every day, squeezing his legs, smacking his bottom, tapping his head, and brushing himself all over.

With five-and six-year-olds, an occasional activity in both literacy and math is to have the children work in partners, and writing on each other's back. Post a set of letters, numbers, or shapes (perhaps five) so the children can see them while they sit in partners—one behind the other facing the same way. One child draws the figures, one at a time, and the child drawn on has to tell which letter (or shape or number) it is. If you do this partner work, try to be the partner of the child whose proprioception is weak.

Some years I've had feely-bags to be used for various areas of study. I place a few plastic letters, coins, or pattern blocks into a cloth bag, and the child has to feel the objects, one a time, and name them before pulling them out of the bag. Also, this can be made more difficult by adding more items—maximum of six—and by timing the activity.

Twirl and Point

With the child, identify the name of several things on a wall—shelf, picture, book leaning on it, light, window. Have the child stand with her back to the wall, three or four feet away, with dominant arm outstretched in front of her. When you say, for example, "Window," she has to quickly turn and point to the window. She must cross her midline as she turns (a right-armed person will need to turn to the left).

Make it more difficult by doing it faster or with smaller objects. Kids can do this in partners, but they first need to be trained by you. They still may not always be able to cross their midline; in any case, it's good reinforcement of left and right, and they'll be more fluent about directionality.

This is a good activity to train parents to do.

Vertical Tracking

Vertical tracking lists are narrow strips about 2 inches by 11½ inches on which I've typed or drawn a repeating series of pictures or letters. You can make the picture yourself with small stickers in random order.

The task of the child is first to read down the list; then, with a pointer or her finger, touch all the pictures or letters you designate. "Touch all triangles," you might say. This task is timed, and the child tries to beat her own time.

A variant of this task is as follows: use a worksheet with the letters of the alphabet placed in order but with many other numerals included. (You can make these worksheets, but they're commercially available.)

There may be five or six lines of letters in a grid of perhaps 50 or 60 items, and the child has to touch and read the letters in order, working the lines top to bottom. Also this is a useful exercise for horizontal tracking practice, but in this case, the child reads the lines across the worksheet.

What's Missing? (Requires a partner)

Place six different items in the middle of a table—paper clip, walnut, rubber band, pencil, hair clip, etc. One child studies the items for a minute or so. Tell her to close her eyes and say if she can see all six items in her mind. If she can't, tell her to look at them again, then close her eyes. While her eyes are closed, her partner removes one item from the set. Ask her to open her eyes and tell what item is missing.

Make this task more difficult by doing the following: try putting seven items out, then eight; take two away; add another one, so instead of the child saying what's missing, she will say what's new.

XES (This is a two-person activity)

Use stiff paper XES made of two, two-by-twelve-inch strips stapled together into an X shape. The best paper for this purpose is old file folders, but lightweight

cardboards works well too. Cut the strips as straight as possible to eliminate distracting waves or wiggles.

One child holds the X at chest height, the other stands facing her about three feet away. With one arm pointing at her partner, straight and stiff from the shoulder, she "traces" the X shape in the air about a foot away from it. The shape the child will make is actually an "8" lying on its side, also known as the infinity symbol.

After 15 tracings of Xes with one arm, the child does 15 with the other arm. Then the partners switch roles. Each partner gets two turns in each role. Brain Gym® variants of this activity are: "Elephant Ears" and "Lazy Eights".

Section Three

What I've Learned about Movement and Vision

When I first arrived in Seattle, Washington in 1990, I met Anne Green Gilbert. I read her book, *Teaching the Three Rs Through Movement Experiences.* This book reflects Gilbert's 1977 to 1978 work using dance activities to enhance and embed language arts concepts with third graders.

Her students' scores on standardized tests went up thirteen percent, while in the same time frame, the district average decreased twenty-five percent. I began to use her ideas with my students from Grade 1 to graduate school.

In 1996, I first learned of Brain Gym® from another reading teacher. I bought the books, *Brain Gym* and *Brain Gym for Teachers,* and I included them in my work with unsuccessful readers. The Brain Gym® exercises are excellent ways to improve the cross-lateral connections necessary for reading and learning. I integrated them into my routine with my readers that had the most needs. You can view a sample of BrainGym® by scanning the QR code with your smart phone or typing www.youtube.com/watch?v=VL4an7UC3wA into your browser.

In the summer of 1999, I took a class with Bette Lamont, Director of Developmental Movement Consultants in Seattle. She uses movement and exercises to help children whose neurological patterns are not complete or have been interrupted. Her clients also include brain-injured people that need to reconnect themselves after car accidents and strokes.

In her work, Bette Lamont sees many of the same kinds of problems of focus and balance that I was seeing in ordinary kids. I learned from her how to work with these kids in new ways.

Finally, in 2001, I met Dr. Nancy Torgerson, a developmental optometrist, and I learned about how vision works. In particular, I learned that having 20/20 vision has almost nothing to do with it. I began to understand what my students need in addition to phonics, fluency, and writing practice to become literate and whole.

This section presents my most important learnings about movement, vision, neurodevelopment patterns, and human growth.

In the *Pathways* Spring 1996 edition, Bette Lamont, Developmental Movement therapist wrote in her article "Learning and Movement", "The nervous system of each new human being must go through a definite series of developmental stages…as the baby programs his motor/perceptual equipment, nerves, and brain cells by using his whole body and all of his senses." She continued, "Babies are driven to move from the day they're born, crawling, creeping, rolling, reaching. As our babies move, reflex activities feed information to the brain, integrating its functions and giving the infants information about themselves and their world. When they are moving, they come to understand the visual, auditory, and tactile elements of their world. They integrate an understanding of pain, of touch, of sequence, distance, closeness, and of life."

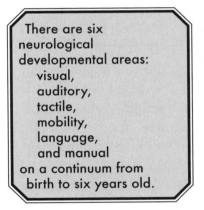

> There are six neurological developmental areas:
> visual,
> auditory,
> tactile,
> mobility,
> language,
> and manual
> on a continuum from birth to six years old.

Tactile (loosely having to do with touch) and Vestibular (loosely having to do with balance) are part of these areas. As a human develops during the first six years of life, there are milestones, skills building on each other to develop a "finished" human with all systems working well. At the beginning of a child's life outside the womb, the sections of the brain called the Medulla and the Pons, (also known as the reptilian brain), are in action. These sections of the brain are the most primitive. At first, they operate only by reflex: the response to light, the random movements of arms and legs, crying, the Babinski reflex, the startle reflex, and the grasp reflex. They are automatic responses, and they're a baby's means of connecting to the world (on average) for the first month.

> The big umbrella areas of development are:
> mobility,
> sensory integration,
> vision, and
> language.

During the next stage (on average, three to six months) another section of the lower brain, the Pons, activates and the baby begins more purposeful responses to heat, cold, pain, and hunger and movement. The baby begins to crawl when on his stomach, and he is able to more clearly see shapes. Horizontal eye movements begin here. When the baby moves across the floor, he will be one-sided first and then become cross lateral when he moves.

At approximately seven months, the Midbrain engages, and the baby begins to discriminate sound and more detail in vision, begins to creep on hands and knees, begins to make his own sounds with a purpose and adds vertical eye movement in order to see where he's going.

Between six and eighteen months as the Cortex becomes more engaged, the baby is able to differentiate sounds as words, can see with depth perception, has a tactile sense, which conveys three-dimensionally, and he can balance upright. Between eighteen months and six years, virtually all the work of the developing human occurs in the cortical areas of the brain; many areas are "finished," among them talking, walking, sidedness, tactile differentiation, and writing. All the sophisticated elements of being a human should be in place.

The development of the body, brain, limbic system (our social/emotional connections) happen together—

Carla Hannaford, author of *Smart Moves* (Great Ocean Publishers 1995, pg 18) wrote, "Learning proceeds as we interact with the world." She continued, "In the brain and body, this learning takes the form of communication among neurons. As we receive sensory stimuli and initiate movements, our neurons form extensions called dendrites to other neurons. Dendritic extensions bring the nerve cells into communication with other nerve cells. Neuronal groups form patterns of communication that become pathways, and with use, superhighways, through which we easily access and act upon world. The process of nerve cell connecting and networking is, in reality, learning and thought."

> The brain's balance system is called the vestibular system, and the body has to be in balance or many of our other systems will not work as they should–

The proprioceptive system consists of hearing, vision, and the sense-of-where-you-are-in space. It relies on the body being in balance in order to function. Rolling, jumping, spinning, swinging, twirling, and dancing are activities that help to build and finish the vestibular system, as children grow through the first two years and beyond.

Today, most elementary schools no longer have swings on their playgrounds. Most schools have abandoned the whirling platforms that kids could run beside to leap on, simply to ride or go around in an orbit that required their eyes and bodies to constantly reorient themselves as they traveled.

Where do children now get that experience of swinging and spinning? They certainly won't get it while sitting in front of their video games. The removal of swinging equipment from playgrounds is now universal in the United States because of concern about possible injuries to children's bodies. But without swinging and spinning equipment in the playgrounds, there is greater possibility of injury to brain development.

By the age of five, children should have determined their sidedness–

When children color or reach to pick up things, they will use only their right or their left hands, not both interchangeably. In first grade, if a child is still using both hands, I'm not above "helping" the child to choose one hand to use. This rarely happens, but it's paralyzing to the child's progress not to have his sidedness determined. I use "his" advisedly here because it's most often the male children who are in this stage.

Becoming aware of and using the sides of the body independently is a significant developmental pattern. Also it's an inevitable developmental pattern because the connectors between hemispheres, a large mass of nerve fibers (200-300 million) called **the corpus callosum,** will grow and develop as part of the transition to the cross-lateral pattern, after the body-side pattern is well established. As is the case in many areas of human growth, a boy's corpus callosum develops later than a girl's will develop.

There was a time when left-handedness was considered inferior. The damage done to children who were forced to change their handedness is incalculable. Fortunately today, changing handedness is no longer done.

> The strongest diagnostic tool for determining finished or unfinished developmental patterns is the crawl–

When a human can crawl on her tummy, reaching up and out with an arm as the opposite leg bends and pushes away with its toes, and continue this pattern of movement across a smooth floor surface, I say she very likely "finished". If she still can't read or still has social problems or doesn't like herself, it is, for me, not because she has movement and patterning issues.

> Vision and sight are not the same thing because vision doesn't happen in the eyes. Vision happens in the brain–

This misunderstanding is responsible for most if not all of the missed diagnoses of children's vision needs. "*Sight* is merely what results from the eye's response to light shining into it. *Vision* results from the child actively interpreting and understanding the information made available through the eyes," explains Nancy Torgerson, Doctor of Optometry in Lynnwood, Washington. Many children have 20/20 eyesight, which is the measure of focus at distance, yet many of these children have vision problems.

The usual eye screening in public school or at the pediatrician's office doesn't measure visual efficiency, which are the ways the eyes are meant to work.

Visual efficiency means how well the eyes fixate (look), follow (track), fuse (coordinate together), and focus (make objects clear).

—Dr. Lynn F. Hellerstein, *See It Say It Do It*

The Snellen chart in the school nurse's office is the big chart with all the E's going in various directions. This chart only measures visual acuity, which is the ability to see tiny details in the distance, for example the classroom chalkboard.

In 1862, a doctor named Snellen developed this chart to check the vision abilities of young Union soldiers. If the soldier could see 20/20 on the Snellen's chart, he was sent off to fight in the Civil War.

"If your child sees 20/20, he wins," writes Cook. "If he cannot see 20/20, he loses and gets glasses. Unfortunately, the child with 20/20 acuity may win the battle only to lose the war." (Cook, *When Your Child Struggles,* Invision Press, 1992, pg. 34)

The battle against poor eyesight is still being fought in much the same way as it was fought during the Civil War.

—David Cook, *When Your Child Struggles*

This is not to say it's not important for my students and me to be able to see the chalkboard or for the Confederate and Union soldiers to see each other or anyone licensed to drive to see street signs.

Of all the children in Section One, only two wore glasses for seeing the chalkboard. Typically, at the least two children in grades K-4 appropriately wear glasses to see the chalkboard, and IT IS THEIR ONLY PROBLEM.

For those with the other vision issues (as with Amina in Section One), glasses to correct for distance only correct for distance. In order to help these children see as they need to see in order to read and cope with their lives, vision therapy may be not only useful but essential. A behavioral or developmental optometrist should assess these children.

> The two big areas of concern are teaming and tracking–

I think about eyes when elementary students, ages 6-10, are having trouble reading, and yet they seem to have the BrainDance in pretty good shape, and they can crawl in an acceptably cross patterned way.

I've learned about and know to watch for two big areas of concern—*teaming and tracking.*

Tracking is reading from one side of the page of print to the other (horizontal), and from the top of the page to the bottom (vertical) without skipping any letters, words, or lines and with a smooth rhythm. I'm assuming that the text is age and ability appropriate. Tracking exercises are easy, fun, and generally bring good success.

Teaming is the convergence of the two eyes so that the binocularity required is available to the child. Teaming is more difficult to identify and correct. There are some exercises, which won't hurt, but a child with eye-teaming issues requires some professional intervention from a developmental optometrist.

To find developmental optometrists in your area, scan the QR code with your smart phone or in your browser

go to covd.org and type in your zip code in the search feature. When you find one, ask if the office has a parent information meeting, which is usually held in the evening. Attend the meeting and learn about what a child's vision should be. (See Appendix C for a checklist for parents and teachers of elementary school children.)

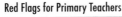

Twelve ways (at the least) the eyes need to work beyond acuity:

Eye Movement Control (Tracking)

Focusing

Visual Discrimination

Form Perception and Reproduction

Figure-Ground Perception

Visual Imagery

Eye-Hand Coordination

Visual Closure

Laterality and Directionality

Auditory-Visual Interaction

Vestibular Function

Eye-Teaming

Many problems in Section One of this book are due to a lack in one or more of the areas listed above, and none of them is measured by the usual "vision screening" at school. (See Appendix B for a more complete definition of these eye behaviors.)

Anne Green Gilbert, Director of the Creative Dance Center, also wrote in 2001, "Moving through these patterns over time may help us fill in any missing gaps in our neurological development due to birth trauma, illness, environment, head injury, or not enough "tummy time" as a baby."

> The BrainDance is based on the developmental movement patterns human beings move through in the first year of life to wire the central nervous system so that the brain can operate at its full potential.
>
> 
>
> creativedance.org.

Gilbert outlines eight patterns:

Breath

Tactile

Core-Distal

Head-Tail

Upper-Lower

Body-Side

Cross-Lateral

Vestibular

Every morning, my class does BrainDance, and every time, I get an *ahaa*! or two.

As with any other activity, it's important to vary how to do the patterns. Sometimes I lead; sometimes I turn on

> BrainDance is an effective way to quickly review the developmental patterns.

the BrainDance CD, which has another voice naming the patterns; sometimes I have BrainDance leaders (this is a classroom job). Some days, we do the BrainDance in six minutes; some days it takes twelve (12) or so minutes.

Every week, I change up how we do BrainDance because the brain needs variety in order to continue to make growth. Each week, I choose from the fifteen (15) dance concepts in Anne Green Gilbert's book, *Creative Dance for All Ages.*

A large chart of these dance concepts is posted on the door. It's the BrainDance leaders' job to put a sticker next to the concept we're using that week.

For some reason, if we haven't done BrainDance (an early assembly, a field trip, etc.), the children usually get squirrelly later in the day. Often I stop and say, "We're pretty squirrelly." And invariably, a child will say, with a certain degree of smugness, "Mrs. Johnson. This morning, we didn't do the BrainDance!" (See BRAINDANCE in Appendix A for detailed directions and script, as well as the supporting rationale and background.)

Human crawling is the cross-lateral walking pattern on the floor. Most babies crawl as they develop normally.

> *Human progress usually makes new human problems.*
>
> —Anonymous

Today, many American children don't have the time to crawl around on their tummies either because their mothers are afraid to have them on their tummies or because they're too busy and keep their babies in a more restrained spot on the floor.

Often, floors are carpeted, and it's difficult to impossible to crawl on carpeting. There's nowhere in the house for the child to develop her cross-lateral pattern!

Children's Play has Changed.

We used to say, "Play is the child's work." When a young child played with his environment and the other beings in it, he learned social cues, weight and measurement, the way his body works, the way weather works, and nearly everything else.

When the child came to school, at five, six, or seven years old, all the teacher really had to do was help him categorize his learning, help him arrange the world so that it made sense, and help him to describe it with words and numbers.

The child was already a scientific investigator, collecting data, experimenting with trial and error, and constantly drawing and revising conclusions about how the world worked, and he'd fit into it. He was actively participating in his own development. "Nature," says Jane Healy in *Endangered Minds,* (Simon & Schuster, 1998, pg. 82), "provides a schedule for natural maturation. A healthy brain stimulates itself by active interaction with what is finds challenging and interesting in its environment."

Hellerstein reports on a 2005 Kaiser Family Foundation study, which found average screen time of four hours, per day. Video games can lead to poor social skills. "There is little or no movement with most. Players are stationary. [*There is not social interaction.* —KJ]. (Hellerstein, *See It. Say It. Do It.,* HiClear, Publishing, 2110, pg 100).

I love the pictures Jane Healy draws in, *Failure to Connect, (*Simon & Schuster, 1998) of two children playing video games together. They are *playing,* and they are *together* in the same physical space with their controllers in their hands mere inches from each other, but they are not playing together. They don't look at each other. They don't speak to each other. They give no clues to each other's feelings through body language or words.

Afterword

In 1999 I met a sweet boy, Mario, who couldn't learn to read. He wanted to; his family wanted him to; he had support, not to say entitlement, from all sides. He worked hard, and his teachers and I (the reading teacher) helped him a lot, but Mario was always behind his classmates.

His mom was filled with discouragement when we met at Mario's sixth grade parent-teacher conference. She cried when she asked, "What will happen to Mario when he's in middle school?"

I suggested she take him to a Developmental Movement Center.

"I guess it won't hurt," she said with doubt crossing her face.

Two years later, I accidentally met Mario when he was walking to the bus.

After many smiles, I asked, "Whatever happened when you did that movement therapy?"

Mario stopped still in the middle of the sidewalk, flung out both arms, and he said, "It changed my life."

Mario went on to graduate from high school with good grades. He was president of the student body and starred in many theater productions. Confidence is his middle name. He is *finished,* and he is thriving.

***

Many of the problems I've presented can probably be remedied with simple exercises. When there are deficits and missed moments in natural development because of the pressures, structures, and fears evident in today's society, they perhaps can be made up. I like to think so. I like to hope so.

Appendix A

BrainDance

How To Do BrainDance

For the first two weeks of school I lead to or the BrainDance CD voice leads every day; then the student leaders take over at least three days of the week. Trying not to do the same thing all the time, this is what I may say (always saying the pattern first, always doing the movements myself):

"**Breath:** take a big breath in through your nose and out through your mouth. Put your hand on your tummy so you can feel the breath coming in." Do this at least three times. If the concept is Speed that week I might say, "Take a breath in quickly, in short breaths, and exhale slowly: then breath in slowly and exhale quickly."

"**Tactile:** with your hands squeeze each arm up and down, each leg up and down, your head, your hands, your face, and as much of your backside as you can reach. Then tap all these body parts; then brush from the top of your head all the way to your toes." If the concept is Speed, try the squeezes medium speed, do the tapping fast and the brushing slow.

"**Core-Distal:** Make a big X with your whole body, then curl yourself into as small a ball as you can." Do this five or six times. If the concept is Speed, do a fast explode-to-X and a slow curl; alternate these.

"**Head-Tail:** Now we are like a snake or a worm, moving the spine as many ways as you can. Stay standing: bend forward, bend backward, bend sideways, make a circle with your tail or with your head." If the concept is Speed, do a very shaky quick wiggle and then a slow python-like movement.

"**Upper-Lower:** Glue your feet to the floor and move only your upper body. Swing your arms as many ways as you can, twist like the inside of a washing machine, flop your upper body around and sideways. Don't forget your head! Now we unglue our feet and hold onto the earth with our arms and move our lower body as many ways as we can." Try knee bends, marching, skooching sideways with both feet together; if the concept is Speed, march in place fast for a few seconds, (it will sound like an earthquake) and then tiptoe slowly.

"**Body-Side:** Keep one side of your body still. Do whatever you can with the other side; then switch sides." Practice eye-tracking in this pattern, too: "Hold your thumbs up together in front of you. Move one to the side, watching it go and come back to the middle. Do the same with the other thumb." If the concept is Speed, try swinging one side at medium speed, the other at slow speed. (This will also require and enhance balance.)

"**Cross-Lateral:** touch your right hand to your left ear; touch your left hand to your right ear; now touch opposite shoulders; now knees; now toes. Skip six skips. Skip six skips without moving from your spot." If the concept is Speed, vary the speeds of these crossing movements. These will become more complex as the days go by."Try touching your right hand to your left foot behind you"–this is really hard–"or your left elbow on your right knee"–also very hard.

"**Vestibular:** spin while I count to six; stop; breathe; now spin the other way while I count back to zero. Stop, breathe." Or "Let's do flops: flop your head over frontwards and lift it back straight up six times. Breathe." Grown-ups hate to spin: kids love it. The point of this activity is to be off-balance so that the brain can work to bring you on- balance. Show caution so the children won't fall down. "Be sure you know where your friends are as you spin." I usually don't change the speed of spinning and flopping; it's enough to do it.

WHY Do BrainDance

"There is folk dance in every culture and group on the earth, and every folk dance uses these eight patterns," explains Anne Green Gilbert."People have always instinctively known they need all the patterns." Gilbert identifies eight developmental patterns in the growth of human s from birth to five.

Breath: Everything about life and movement rides on breath. Breathing is the first thing the baby does upon its emergence from the womb, and breathing is what we keep on doing. There is such a thing as "cellular breath," which I think I believe in although I can't imagine it. Breathing connects the new human to the world. Breathing allows us to sense our selves and our world. The body's trunk is a cylinder expanding in all directions.

Tactile: This word comes from the Latin for "touching." It is in the tactile pattern that awareness of where the body is in space (proprioception) and connection of the five senses to the child's world (sensory integration) belong. Tactile is about bonding. The tactile connections can happen before birth, as the baby bumps the sides of the uterus and is bathed in its fluids; the first important tactile sensation for the infant is being squeezed through the birth canal.

The tactile realm is also the beginning of socialization: before you can reach out to others, you need to know where your edges and boundaries are. Bonding is the result of tactile stimulation at the beginning of the baby's life. Tummy time grounds the baby to the earth and allows her to explore outward, connecting to her world, sensing the parts of her body and reaching out to others.

Core-Distal: The startle reflex is the first embodiment of the core-distal pattern. This is the pattern of reaching out, with all six ends of the body (head, tail, fingers, and toes) and curling back into the center or core; in this pattern we alternate the intrapersonal, or self, with the interpersonal, or our environment. The Core-Distal pattern establishes both the kinesphere (the distal reach), and its center (the core muscles).

Head-Tail: The spine is the window to the mind and allows the body's expressivity, keeping the body in constant interactive relationship with itself and the world. Body attitude is determined by head-tail movements, and the three sections of the spine (cervical, thoracic, and lumbar) allow for movements in various planes (horizontal, vertical, and sagittal).

Upper-Lower: The lower body allows for stability in order for mobility to occur, and vice versa. The pelvis is the power source and center of gravity, supporting the weight of the body. Walking is initiated in the trunk of the body. The upper body provides mobility in order for stability to occur, connecting things and people. Function and expression work together; both the lower and the upper body reach for goals and set boundaries.

Body-Side: The body-side pattern balances development and musculature on both sides of the body and spine. Dominant and non-dominant sidedness are determined. Eye-tracking competence comes in the body-side pattern, as does the beginning of understanding life's polarities and choices: yes/no, can/can't, work/play, right/left, black/white, right/wrong. This stage continues the patterns of socialization, both reaching out to others and deciding what is important for yourself.

Cross-Lateral: The cross-lateral pattern is the integration of the right and left brains, vertical eye-tracking, the fully connected front, back, and quadrants of the body, and the cortical connections of the fully engaged brain.

And finally**, Vestibular**: Is it the eighth pattern? Or the 6th sense–or first of all? The vestibular system begins in the second month after conception. It provides our relationship to gravity and controls movement because it controls balance: to go OFF balance is to find where you are ON balance. There is a relationship between the vestibular system and the work of the eyes.

The Cross-Lateral pattern is the pattern unique to humans. We're also the species which walks upright all the time, as opposed to bears and kangaroos that occasionally walk upright, or with serious assistance from their tails. The same is true for dinosaurs that occasionally walked upright with assistance from their tails. The word "cross-lateral" is when the body uses its opposite sides in coordination with the upper and lower body in its locomotion–"lateral" is from the Latin word for "side."

When a human walks, the right arm and the left leg move forward together, then the left arm and the right leg move forward. Walking is the alternation of these movements. The walking human is moving in the horizontal and vertical planes simultaneously, and balancing as well. The easiest direction to move in is forward; six- and seven-year-olds can walk in a cross-lateral walk in a forward direction, most of them in a finished way. Moving backward is much less safe, not as easy, and nowhere near as automatic.

The Cross-lateral pattern, then, integrates all the others. It requires awareness of sidedness, automaticity with balance, and the ability to move in all the planes a body can move in: vertical, horizontal, sagittal. The body accommodates diagonal movement, and all four quadrants of the body can be and are engaged by cross-lateral movement. The right and left sides of the brain are also integrated in the cross-lateral pattern.

Appendix B

Twelve Ways the Eyes Need to Work

Eye Movement Control: When you are looking at something, you have to be able to stay on it long enough for your brain to take it in. When you are reading, your eyes can't skip or hop irregularly from word to word, back and forth. Tracking exercises can help with this, as can the Twirl and Point activity.

Focusing: In school as in life–think of a soccer field! Or just crossing the street—your eyes have to be able to shift focus without delays or blurring, from near to far distances and in between. Eye muscles are amazingly quick when they are working; if they are not, refocusing is not automatic.

Visual Discrimination: Many letters (fewer numbers) can be confusingly alike when a child first begins to use them. Differences among pictures, letters, words, and for adults phone numbers, signs, and faces must be readily identified and discriminated quickly, as automatically as possible.

Form Perception and Reproduction: This is about printing correctly; drawing shapes in math; identifying similar words and pictures. What does a letter or a number or a shape or a sign look like? How do I see it correctly, identify it correctly, and make it correctly every time?

Visual Figure-Ground Perception: This is about foreground and background, and by extension depth perception. Sometimes the wall-huggers have this problem, and can't really tell where the wall is. Children with Figure-Ground problems may have trouble interpreting graphs and pictures, finding a chart on the wall, or distinguishing main idea from subordinating ideas in a text.

Visual Imagery: Visual imagery and visual memory are essential in recalling patterns and spellings and sequences in all school areas.

Eye-hand Coordination: You have to be able to see what it is you are doing with your hands, whether it is a school activity like reading or a home activity like making your bed and putting away your toys. The label of "clumsy" is often used of people at any age with coordination problems; these problems are equally as likely to reflect a vision problem as a motor one.

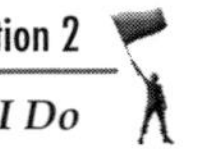

Visual Closure: It's important to see the whole of what you are looking at and working with. This skill often goes along with Visual Imagery–if you can't see a shape as a whole you won't be able reproduce that shape.

Laterality and Directionality: Right and Left. Up and Down. Forward and Backward. Crossing the midline. Turning the right way. Following directions. Finding things. Reading maps and charts and graphs. This skill is linked to proprioception–where are you in space (see Vestibular, below).

Auditory-Visual Integration: Can a child process auditory information and match it to what is seen? When you read aloud, can the child make pictures in her head in order to comprehend what she is hearing?

Vestibular Function: It's essential to understand that the body operates in three dimensions and integrates them. When a child goes off balance without intending to, it's very possible the eyes are not seeing enough to effectively provide that orientation. The vestibular system provides a means for the body to know where it is in space in order for the body to be safely oriented and stable.

Eye Teaming: Last but first, do the child's eyes work together? Are both eyes focusing on the retina in such a way that there is only one, correct, image for the brain to interpret, for the brain to "see?" A "no" to this question will make all the other skills very nearly impossible to achieve.

Appendix C

Does a Child Need Vision Therapy?

Here is a checklist (modified from the Optometric Extension Program Foundation's (www.oep.org) checklist distributed to educators by many optometrists) which may help you make up your mind.

Eye-movement abilities (Ocular Motility)

____ His head turns as he reads across a page

____ He loses the place frequently when reading

____ He has a short attention span in reading or writing

____ He re-reads or skips lines

Eye-teaming abilities (Binocularity)

____ She repeats letters within words

____ She omits letters, numbers, or phrases

____ She misaligns numbers in columns

____ She squints, closes, or covers one eye

____ She tilts her head extremely while reading

____ She turns her head so only one eye focuses on the print

Visual form perception (Visual Imagery)

____ He fails to recognize the same word in the next sentence

____ She reverses letters and/or words in writing and copying

____ He has difficulty recognizing minor differences

____ She confuses words with similar beginnings and endings

____ She cannot visualize what is read, silently or aloud

Eye-Hand Coordination Abilities

____ She repeatedly confuses left-right directions

____ He misaligns both horizontal and vertical series of numbers

____ She places words or drawings on the page oriented incorrectly.

____ He writes crookedly, with poor spacing, and can't stay on the lines.

Appendix D

My Assessments

1. Make a paper eyeball (or use a pencil-sized stick with a one-inch blobby thing on the eraser end). Hold this tracking device about twelve inches in front of the person and slowly move it across the person's field of vision from left to right. If the person moves his/her head, put a beanbag on it (if a reminder doesn't keep it still).The eyes should move evenly back and forth, tracking the object/eyeball. Do this four times, taking about five seconds to go in each direction each time. If the person complains that it hurts or if you see the eyes watering, that's one red flag; if the person's eyeballs do a little jump about half-way across, that's another. Do the same thing only up and down for vertical tracking.

2. With a ball-point pen, put a small dot on the side of the eraser of an ordinary pencil. Hold it in front

of the person about a foot away. Tell the person that the eyes will probably cross as you move the pencil, and tell children that it might tickle. (Sometimes children start to giggle during this test.) Tell them to keep focused on the dot. Bring the pencil toward the nose in two seconds, back it off, wait two seconds, repeat twice more. If the eyes cross (and the kid giggles) things are probably okay; if the eyes do not cross at all or if, when the pencil is almost to the nose, one of the eyes slides or jumps sideways, that is a big red flag.

3. The screening I put together for all the kindergarten children is similar in structure to the health screening most elementary schools do every year, with the school nurse or parents at stations taking height, weight, and checking for 20/20 vision with a variant of the "Big E" Snellen chart. I get parents and briefly train them using the directions they will have at their stations. The assessments 1 and 2 above are part of the screening.

K-1 Vision Screening

Child________________ Date ________ Age ___

1. Tracking the eyeball — circle one

Horizontal:

smooth and even   bumpy   unable to do

Needed beanbag on head: yes   no

Vertical:

smooth and even   bumpy   unable to do

2. Balance — do twice, record how many seconds

Eyes open right foot ________

Eyes open left foot ________

Eyes closed right foot ________

Eyes closed left foot __________

3. Teaming—with pencil eraser do twice

smooth wiggly/jerky
eyes together L or R moves

4. Skipping

yes gallop mixed

5. Visual Discrimination _____correct of 12

works quickly works slowly

uses finger to track

6. Tummy crawl

X-pat elbows drag leg L or R
no legs on side

Comments

____

____

____

____

____

____

____

Instructions For Volunteers for Eye Screening

(I print and mount these on separate sheets for the different stations)

Tracking the eyeball

Horizontal: Ask the child to look at the eyeball (you are holding it at about a foot from her face) and follow it with her eyes as you slowly move it across the field of vision—take a slow count of 5 to get across one way. Go back the other way. Do this twice. Watch the child's eyes.

If she moves her head, tell her you are going to put the (beanbag or beanie dog) on her head to keep it still. "Bumpy" means that the eyes jiggle as they move along the horizontal track, especially in the middle. "Unable" means that the child's eyes stay focused on the beginning of the track and don't follow the eyeball.

Vertical: Ask the child to focus on the eyeball as you move it up and down in front of him, a slow count of 5 each direction.

1. Balance

Ask the child to cross arms over chest (demonstrate) and stand on one foot as long as he can. Count slowly by seconds. If the child gets to 10, say WOW and go on. Do both feet, eyes open first then closed.

2. Teaming

Tell the child you are going to do something that may make her eyes feel a little tickly and her eyes will probably cross. Put a small dot on the side of the eraser at the end of an ordinary pencil. Hold it in front about a foot away. Tell her to keep focused on the dot. Bring the pencil toward the nose in two seconds. Say, "Good. We're going to do that again. Ready?" It may happen that the eyes do begin to cross and then one of them slides off. Note which one if so.

3. Skipping

Have the child skip to the end of the hall—20 feet or so—and back. Say, "Good!" even if it wasn't skipping. If you're not sure, ask him to do it again.

4. Visual Discrimination (use the same sheet for all–they don't mark it)

Put the first sheet in front of the child saying, "Look at the first picture and find one in this row that is exactly the same." Cover the sheet from the bottom as you work.

Put the second sheet in front of the child saying, "Look at the first picture and find the one in this row that is NOT the same." Cover the sheet from the bottom as you work.

5. Tummy Crawl

Ask the child to get down on her tummy on the linoleum (about 8 feet of it).Tell her to go to the other end of it, keeping her tummy on the floor, and she may use any arms and legs she needs to do so. Return the same way.

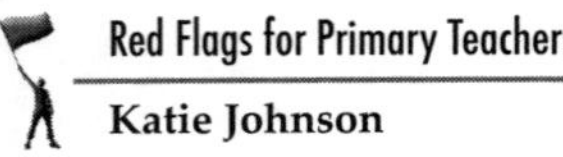
Red Flags for Primary Teachers
Katie Johnson

Other Neurodevelopmental Assessments

Tactile

A dead giveaway for children who have some tactile and probably proprioception problems is that they can't stand to be touched by a tag in their shirt or by pants that are scratchy, such as jeans. Almost always such children wear sweatpants to school and don't like to have their shirts tucked in.

I try to ascertain if and where the child's sidedness has settled, by doing the Tactile assessment developed by the Northwest Neurodevelopmental Training Center:

Ask the child to stand in front of you with her arms stretched out palms up and her eyes closed. Tell her you will touch a spot on her arm, and she must touch the same spot using her other hand. Do this, touching her arm on six different spots from thumb to elbow. If she can touch your spot within 1/4 inch, she is probably okay and her two hemispheres are communicating (across the corpus callosum) to help her understand where she is in space. If not, she will need a great many patterning and midline exercises and probably some occupational therapy or neurological repatterning to move her along.

Crawling

A child by age three should be able to crawl on her tummy using both arms and both legs with equal strength and in an alternating cross-patterned way, with her tummy on the floor throughout and her head turning from side to side as she crawls. If this is not the case, practice the Scarecrow and crawling on a smooth (tile, wood, or linoleum) surface often, every day, for ten minutes at a time.

Balance

Because the vestibular system is fundamental to everything else, and because it is so hard to understand, children can never have too much vestibular practice (the removal of swings from playgrounds is a grave offense against children's development).The easiest practice is to do the balance activity described in the VISION SCREENING section above. If you keep track of how long the children can do this balancing (and make hooray noises for each additional second), you should see some improvement over time. This helps with proprioception, too, and it can also be easily done at home.

Glossary

ADHD	Attention Deficit Hyperactivity Disorder
Bicameral	using both sides of the body and the brain
Body-Side pattern	see Appendix A
BrainDance	see Appendix A
Convergence	the muscles of both eyes work together
Corpus callosum	nerve fibers connecting the two hemispheres of the brain
Crawl	move on the stomach using both arms and both legs
Creep	move on hands and knees
Cross-lateral pattern	see Appendix A

Developmental patterning	working through the developmental patterns to be sure their work is finished
Finished	when neurodevelopment is complete
Midline	imaginary line dividing the body vertically
Neurodevelopment	the growth and coordination of the motor, tactile, vestibular and vision systems
Pre-cortical	areas of the brain that develop before the cortex
Proprioception	awareness of where the body is in space
Sidedness	dominance of right or left side
Sound-symbol correspondence	the relationship between letters and the sounds they make
Tactile	touch
Teaming	convergence of the eyes
Vestibular	system that controls the sense of movement and balance
Vision therapy	optometry work that develops and improves visual skills and abilities

Bibliography

Barry, Susan R. (2009) *Fixing My Gaze: A Scientist's Journey into Seeing in Three Dimensions*. New York: Basic Books.

Benoit, Robin with Jillian Benoit. (2010) *Jillian's Story: How Vision Therapy Changed My Daughter's Life*. Dallas: The P 3 Press.

Cook, David L., O.D. (1992) *When Your Child Struggles: The Myths of 20/20 Vision, What Every Parent Needs to Know.*_Atlanta: Invision Press.

Doidge, Norman. (2007) *The Brain That Changes Itself: Stories of Personal Triumph from the Frontiers of Brain Science*. New York: Penguin Books.

Gilbert, Anne Green. (2006) *Brain-Compatible Dance Education.* Reston, VA: National Dance Association.

__________. (1992) *Creative Dance for All Ages: A Conceptual Approach*. Reston, VA: National Dance Association / AAHPERD.

__________. (2002) *Teaching the Three Rs Through Movement Activities: A Handbook for Teachers*. Bethesda MD: NDEO.

Hannaford, Carla. (1995) *Smart Moves: Why Learning is Not All In Your Head*. Alexander, NC: Great Ocean Publishers.

Healy, Jane M. (1999) *Endangered Minds: Why Children Don't Think–and What We Can Do About It* . New York: Simon & Schuster.

__________. (1998) *Failure to Connect: How Computers Affect Our Children's Minds—and What We Can Do About It*. New York: Simon & Schuster.

__________. (2004) *Your Child's Growing Mind, Brain Development and Learning From Birth to Adolescence*. New York: Broadway Books. Third edition.

Hellerstein, Lynn F. (2010) *See It. Say It. Do It. The Parent's and Teacher's Action Guide to Creating Successful Students and Confident Kids*. Centennial, CO: HiClear Publishing.

Hoopes, Ann M. and Stanley A. Applebaum. (2009) *Eye Power, a cutting edge report on Vision Therapy*. Amazon.com.

Jensen, Eric. (1995) *Teaching With the Brain in Mind*. Alexandria, VA: ASCD.

Kaplan, Melvin, M.D. (2006) *Seeing With New Eyes: Changing the Lives of Children with Autism, Asperger Syndrome, and Other Developmental Disabilities Through Vision Therapy*. London: Jessica Kingsley Publishers.

Randolph, Shirley L and Heiniger, Margot C. (1994) *Kids Learn From the Inside Out: How to Enhance the Human Matrix*. Boise, ID: Legendary Publishing Company.

REFRENCES FOR TEACHERS

ARTICLES

Scott, Susan. *A Story Unto Itself: Vestibular Stimulation and Eye Movement.* (1995) Portland, OR: Northwest Neurodevelopmental Training Center.

ELECTRONIC MEDIA AND WEBSITES

sidscenter.org/Statistics.html

cdc.gov/nchs/fastats/delivery.htm

cdc.gov/nchs/data/databriefs/db35.pdf

visionhelp.com

pavevision.org

projectfirststep.com

wellnesscke.net/k12.htm

stanleygreenspan.com

pavevision.org

covd.org

alderwoodvisiontherapy.com

themlrc.org

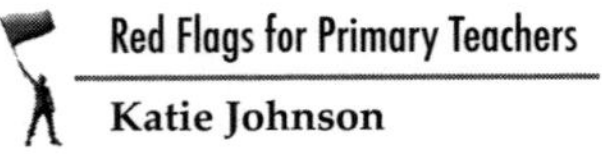

Red Flags for Primary Teachers
Katie Johnson

About Katie Johnson

For many years, Katie Johnson believed that grammar and languages were the most fascinating part of her life, and teaching children to write was her focus as a teacher. For the past fifteen years that fascination has been edged aside by learning about developmental movement and vision and how they affect the lives of her primary-age public school students.

Teaching French in the Philippines for a year was Katie Johnson's first teaching position after graduating from Vassar College, with a major in English and strong minors in Russian and Greek. After teaching two years in high schools, Katie moved into the elementary grades, discovering in 1973 that first grade is where her heart is. Katie has taught first grade, in both Maine and Washington, for 37 of the 46 years she has been a teacher.

Katie Johnson

Katie Johnson has three published books about teaching writing to young children. She has worked as an adjunct professor of literacy in the teacher-training programs of Pacific Oaks College (California) and University of Washington (Bothell campus), as well as in the graduate school of Lesley University (Cambridge, Massachusetts), and done many professional development presentations across the United States. She is a Fellow of the Southern Maine Writing Project and co-teaches an Institute for the Puget Sound Writing Project.

Katie teaches in the Shoreline School District and lives with her partner (also a primary teacher) in an old Craftsman house in Seattle. She likes to dance, read, cook, garden, write, talk, go to the symphony, and sample the ever-evolving microbrew production in the Northwest. She has two daughters, three granddaughters, and two great-grandchildren.